Advance Reviews

"What an interesting perspective - telling the story of Falmouth's history through its historic bells. Peal's Bells of Falmouth is written with a refreshingly creative focus that offers the reader history from a different angle. I found myself anxious to get to the next chapter to discover what the next bell's story would be."
**Ed Haddad, Falmouth Historical Commission,
Falmouth, MA**

"Bells of Falmouth is an adventure story, a mystery, and a history lesson rolled into one entertaining narrative. Peal takes readers along on his quest to identify the bells which once summoned Falmouth residents to church and school, or rang out in times of danger and celebration. His journey takes him into belfries, basements, bucket trucks and fire stations. Along the way, he uncovers fascinating stories of everyday life in bygone years, and why these neighborhood bells were so fondly remembered by many who heard them."
**Meg Costello, Research Manager,
Falmouth Museums on the Green, Falmouth, MA**

"This meticulously researched book contains not only information about the bells of Falmouth, but also extensive histories of local churches, schools and communities. This is a wonderful read for all lovers of our town's history."
**Colleen Hurter, Archivist and Assistant Director,
Woods Hole Historical Museum, Woods Hole, MA**

"Peal is a natural researcher and when combined with his passion for bells you get this excellent book filled to the brim with fascinating stories and enchanting history."
**William McCarthy, Archivist,
Congregational Library and Archives, Boston, MA**

"Peal's interesting book about bells not only provides a catalog of an important category of historical artifacts, but also presents the social and economic contexts that led to their original acquisition and use. The book helps us to appreciate the heritage of a soundscape that our ancestors knew and that can still be heard to a lesser extent today.
With a chapter about each bell or group of bells plus some background material about bells in general, this book provides excellent coverage of the subject. While I could have wished for more photos of the bells themselves, this lack is more than compensated for by the inclusion of locator maps, tables of essential details, and a listing of the bells' inscriptions.

Altogether, this book is a fine example of what historians elsewhere could do to document and preserve an important but often under-appreciated part of our heritage."

Carl Scott Zimmerman,
Campanologist, Saint Louis, MO

"Peal's book guides readers on an expedition through the captivating historical tapestry of a charming New England town. Employing the resonant symbol of bells, the author ushers us back in time, unveiling chronicles of Falmouth's inhabitants and locales. I wholeheartedly endorse this book, especially for those with an inclination towards the study of bells, churches, or just everyday life as far back as colonial New England."

Rachel Lovett, Executive Director,
Falmouth Museums on the Green, Falmouth, MA

"History can be told a number of ways. There are books about times long past and about conflicts regional and global. Biographies tell us of the history makers. Peal recounts Falmouth history through stories behind its bells - church bells, school bells, bells in town buildings. His stories are a fascinating look at pieces of our history."

John Hough, editor and publisher emeritus,
Falmouth Enterprise, Falmouth, MA

"Peal has done a great job of accumulating stories and pictures about bells in Falmouth. This book, backed by extensive research, puts important history in the hands of present and future generations. It is a splendid addition to the body of Falmouth history."

Neil Goeppinger, bell collector, author and
past-president, American Bell Association

"What a nice addition to Falmouth's historical record. This book covers bells from old churches to modern gardens. Stories about firefighting and fog horns. From bells that we still hear today to those that somehow got lost. I particularly like the details about Lawrence Academy, founded in 1834, now the home of the Chamber of Commerce. A well-researched book and fun to read."

Michael Kasparian, CEO/President,
Falmouth Chamber of Commerce, Falmouth, MA

BELLS OF FALMOUTH

*STORIES FROM A HISTORIC MASSACHUSETTS TOWN,
UNCOVERED BY CURIOSITY ABOUT ITS BELLS*

KEN PEAL

Publisher's Information

ISBN 978-1-953080-43-1

© 2023 by Ken Peal

Contact: Kpeal42@gmail.com

ALL RIGHTS RESERVED

No part of this work covered by the copyright herein may be reproduced, transmitted, stored, or used in any form or by any means graphic, electronic, or mechanical, including but not limited to photocopying, scanning, digitizing, taping, Web distribution, information networks, or information storage and retrieval systems, except as permitted by Section 107 or 108 of the 1976 United States Copyright Act, without the prior written permission of the author.

EBookBakery Books

The bell featured on the cover is the 1884 McShane bell that first stirred the author's curiosity and let to this book.

DEDICATION

To: Michele
My loving and patient wife and excellent editor

Who had never heard of bell stories

Table of Contents

Introduction VII
1. Bells in Falmouth - Hidden Gems of History 1
2. Union Chapel is Now History and So is its Bell 7
3. The Holbrook Bell of Lawrence Academy 11
4. Fog Bells Warned Ships Before Horns Came Into Use 15
5. Spohr Gardens Offers a Spring Escape as well as Artifacts ... 19
6. Churches: A Repository of History 23
7. A Walking Tour of Woods Hole 29
8. The Mystery At North Falmouth Congregational Church .. 35
9. The Mystery Of The Roaming Bell 39
10. Sounding The Alarm In The Early Years Of Firefighting ... 43
11. Bells At St. Barnabas Episcopal Church 47
12. The Lawrence High School Bell at St. Barnabas Church ... 51
13. The Paul Revere Bell of the Congregational Church 55
14. The East Falmouth School Bell - Where is it? 59
15. Bell History and Technology 65
16. Maps and Facts 71
17. Inscriptions on Falmouth bells 77

About the Author 85
References 86
Index 92

Introduction

I didn't set out to be a bell fanatic. I have lived in a house built in 1859 for many years and have come to appreciate the value of historic things including many aspects of Falmouth and New England. When I heard that some parishioners from my church were trying to save and restore the bell from our sister church that had closed 50 years ago, I started asking questions. Chapter 1 explains how I got involved in that project but it doesn't explain my larger interest that led to writing the stories in this book.

My initial interest in bells was probably based on my engineering training and the unusual challenge of bell making. And it didn't hurt that their durability makes them items of historic interest. They may be in a historic building or they may have their own story. Then there are some fascinating traditions related to bells, like "change ringing". People notice my surname and often ask if that was a factor in my interest in bells – I don't think so.

I have a natural impulse to organize things, so I collected information about the many bells in town – their location, size, foundry and age. This began as a casual activity but as I collected more information, I added more columns to the spreadsheet. That led to my asking more questions and checking more sources. Pretty soon I was wading into stories about New England traditions and Falmouth's history. Stories like: a fire that nearly engulfed the town in 1947; the town's development as a summer resort in the 1870s; the 1797 Congregational meeting house that was donated in 1983 to a fledgling Jewish community, now lovingly repurposed as a thriving synagogue. The list continues. In 1821 an ad hoc group started an elementary school for underprivileged students; it lasted for 100 years then was taken over by the town in 1922. Or prominent townsfolk who started a high school in 1835, before it was required by law in Massachusetts. The pride in our diverse background – the importance of parts of town that were once thriving villages with different cultures. We now continue to use the old village names like Hatchville, Davisville or Maravista, to identify parts of Falmouth.

Just for fun I wrote a couple of these stories, each oriented around one of the bells and offered them to our independent local newspaper, the *Falmouth Enterprise*. They were published and I was encouraged to write more. Writing each one was an adventure of discovery – in some cases finding previously unrecorded bells (important to true campanologists), in other cases just reviving some great bits of Falmouth history. My curiosity raised a lot of questions for the bell owners. But some weren't able to tell me much about their bell. So I learned the value of being on the ground – in this case, up in the belfry – to get questions answered. I did numerous dubious climbs to dirty places and made some significant discoveries.

Eventually I wrote 14 such stories – they appear as chapters 1 to 14 in this book. The other chapters offer factual information about bells. Chapter 15, "Bell History and Technology", is included for those who want to learn more about bells in general – things like how they work, how they are made, who makes them. I hope some readers may appreciate this but it is not required reading to enjoy the bell stories. Chapter 16, "Maps and Facts", shows the locations of Falmouth's bells and all the technical details I was able to collect. Chapter 17, "Inscriptions", collects all the bell inscriptions together for quick reference.

In the process of writing the stories I learned about enthusiastic groups that are keeping broader aspects of history alive. I developed an appreciation for small societies throughout New England like the Falmouth Historical Society and the Woods Hole Historical Museum that preserve historic artifacts and stories about much more than just bells. I learned about the serious commitment to historic preservation by the State of Massachusetts that led to the Community Preservation Act of 2000, implemented in Falmouth by our Community Preservation Committee and the Historical Commission.

So, take these stories as something between a less-than-scholarly look at the history of Falmouth's bells and a love letter to the town.

.

1

BELLS IN FALMOUTH
— HIDDEN GEMS OF HISTORY

Quick – how many bells do you think there are in Falmouth? Yes - bells, like church bells. You will probably think of the most famous one - the Paul Revere bell at First Congregational Church.

Many other churches have bells and ring them regularly: St. Barnabas Episcopal, Waquoit Congregational, West Falmouth Methodist, etc. Then there are the in-your-face-but-never-noticed bells at the Marine Park on Scranton Avenue or in Spohr Gardens. And the not-so-obvious ones hidden atop the Chamber of Commerce building or in the Woods Hole School. The pair of bells, named after pioneering biologists Louis Pasteur and Gregor Mendel, are in the tower of the Mary Garden on Eel Pond in Woods Hole. I now have a spreadsheet with about thirty bells in Falmouth - how did I get like this?

It started in 2008 when the celebration of 200 years of Methodism in Falmouth at John Wesley Church led to more interest in things historical. Parishioner Bob Dinsmore reminded the church that although the sister Methodist Church in Woods Hole had been decommissioned and the building sold to the Woods Hole Oceanographic Institution (WHOI) back in 1972, the church's bell still belonged to John Wesley. We knew that the Woods Hole Church was formed in 1884, but looking though our archives were surprised to find original paper documents that recorded the meeting on the 24th of July of that year when a few of the faithful along with Pastor R. H. Dorr gathered to form what was then called the People's Methodist Episcopal Church. The archives also included books recording pastors, members, and baptisms from that time.

And of course, the bell. It was common in those days to have a custom bell made to mark important events like the forming of a new church.

Most such bells have inscriptions that tell their story. In this case the inscriptions are "Henry McShane & Co, Baltimore MD, 1884" on one side and "Peoples M.E. Church, Pastor R.H. Dorr, July 1884" on the other. The bronze bell, cast when the McShane company was only 28 years old, weighs 400 pounds, is 27 inches across at the opening and sounds a D note on the musical scale. Together, the bell and the paper documents we found are important historical artifacts.

The Woods Hole Oceanographic Institution's Visitor Center, formerly the People's Methodist Episcopal Church, often called the Woods Hole Methodist Church. Credit - K. Peal

The author rings the bell from the Woods Hole Methodist Church now installed at John Wesley United Methodist Church. Since this picture was taken we installed a clapper with a lanyard so the bell can be rung in a more conventional way.. Credit - K. Peal

WHOI bought the church building and converted it into a visitor center and gift shop. Unfortunately, in 2011 a roof leak caused by the collapse of the bell support frame was discovered requiring the bell to be removed from its roost atop the building. WHOI employee, Doug Handy who drove the crane that retrieved the bell, took it back to his shop, did some maintenance to the bell, then stashed it safely away and forgot about it. There was some consternation when five years later then-Pastor David Calhoun and several parishioners came looking for their bell at the WHOI warehouse, but it wasn't in the database. But word of mouth works inside WHOI; the bell was located in its hideaway and retrieved.

I came late to this project; my interest was piqued because I worked at WHOI for many years. By the time I got involved, the bell had been located at WHOI and delivered as an immovable object to one of the classrooms in John Wesley Church. It weighed several hundred pounds and didn't come with handles. Then there was the bell's broken support frame and a box of motley, unlabeled parts. And there was no plan for what to do with it all.

We consulted several bell historians and were told to first see if it could still be rung. That would guide our deliberations about what to do with it. Using some mechanical gymnastics, we turned the bell over in the church classroom to stand it upside down so it could be rung by hand. The traditional method of swinging of the bell to make it ring was out of the question - the support frame was in pieces and besides the clapper had rusted away years ago. So, we stood it upside down and hit it with a plain-old carpenter's hammer. For all its 133 years, the bell was intact and still had a clear, resonant tone – and loud. Then we had to turn it over again, so it wouldn't fall on somebody.

An enthusiastic and persistent committee was formed that came up with a plan and got the bell installed by August 2018. Grafton Briggs generously helped us to lift the bell onto its newly repaired frame using his expertise in placing grave stones. The installation is at ground level so the bell can be viewed by all and easily rung on special occasions. We rang it for the first time in at least 50 years at the All Saints Day service in November of that year and it is now in regular use.

That is the short version of the story, but during that time memories of other bells in my life began to surface. A family visit to Philadelphia and the Liberty Bell. A guided tour of the tower and bells of Notre Dame in Paris (long before the fire). My daughter becoming a change ringer at an 800-year-old church in Surrey, UK, during a sabbatical there. A business trip to the former East German town of Leipzig—realizing while enjoying an outdoor café that the church across the square was Thomaskirche, where J. S. Bach was Kapellmeister for many years. It never occurred to me that my family name, Peal, might be part of bells' appeal.

There is wide interest in bells. Specialist websites attract bell discoverers worldwide. Friends often tell me about displays they have seen during their travels: on-the-ground displays of historic bells in Mansfield, Connecticut; Victoria, British Columbia; Titusville Presbyterian in Florida. Extensive renovations of chimes and bells in Haverhill, Massachusetts, and Charlottetown, Prince Edward Island.

I have found bell stories all over Falmouth. Some bells are easy to access, and their inscriptions tell their stories, although getting permission from worried officials to actually visit a bell in its belfry has its challenges. Some bells exist in historical records but the bell itself has been lost. Some are hidden and unused, waiting to be discovered and put on public display. Other bells are visible from the ground but are inaccessible, so hold their secrets a little more closely. In one case recently, a Hamilton Tree Co. bucket truck gave me a ride up to look at the bell on top of the Chamber of Commerce building. But that is a story for another day.

2

Union Chapel Is Now History — And So Is Its Bell

Have you ever heard the bell at the Union Chapel in Falmouth Heights? It's a trick question of course, because the chapel was demolished years ago. When I asked local historian and photographer Donald Fish that question, he went me one better: his father installed the original flooring in the chapel and, ironically, was hired to remove the same flooring just before the building was demolished. Others of us who are less informed would be forgiven for thinking of perhaps the St Thomas Chapel or Menauhant Chapel or Grace Memorial Chapel. There is no bell at the St Thomas Chapel. Grace Memorial Chapel has a bell but it's on Central Avenue, not Falmouth Heights. It was built in 1931 as a replacement for the earlier Menauhant Chapel on the same site.

Union Chapel started as an observatory that was part of a real estate development undertaken in 1870 by some Worcester businessmen before seaside resorts were common. In fact, most of the Falmouth coastline then was occupied with salt works; the town had few tourist amenities. The company, Falmouth Heights Land and Wharf Company, acquired most of the real estate in the Heights and drew up a plan that included house lots, streets, hotels, and parks much like those of a city (Worcester?). Lot sales and building construction were slow initially, and the company sold off its rights in 1878, but their plan is pretty much what we see today. Notice street names like Worcester Court, Quinsigamond Avenue, Quinapoxet Avenue, Wachusett Avenue. And Tower House Road was named after Mr. George Tower, one of the Worcester businessmen whose hotel was located where Mariner's Point Resort is now. Candace Jenkins presents a complete

Union Chapel was built originally as an observatory in 1872.
Credit - Falmouth Public Library, Robert C Hunt Jr, Postcard Collection, Creative Commons.

description of this in *"The Development of Falmouth as a Summer Resort 1850-1900."*[1]

The observatory, built in 1872, occupied the highest point in Falmouth Heights, with views of Vineyard Sound and beach access for the residents. Over the years it served as a general store, a fruit store, unofficial post office, meeting place, and sightseeing venue.[2] Articles in the *Falmouth Enterprise* archives tell us that it frequently hosted sales of homemade baked goods and "fancy articles"[3] in support of The Women's Relief Corps,[4] "the ladies of the ME Church,"[5] and the Ladies Aid Society.[6] Much later (1913), it hosted a meeting of the Woman's Suffrage League.[7]

In 1891, a board of trustees was formed with the purpose of converting the observatory to a chapel —Union Chapel—for nondenominational worship services similar to camp meetings at Martha's Vineyard and elsewhere at the time. The seasonal services featured local and out-of-town preachers as well as organ music and singing and often required the addition of folding chairs to accommodate the crowds. In 1905, the chapel was enlarged to provide seating for 200, and other improvements including the addition of a bell given by a "prominent and public-spirited summer resident."[8]

The moment that the central tower fell during demolition of the Chapel in 1929. Credit - from the collection of Mike Crew, source unknown, used by permission.

By the end of the season however, we learn that the bell in the chapel "did not prove satisfactory."[9] I am not sure what the problem could have been or how they broke the news to the public-spirited summer resident. But by the 1906 season, a new bell was installed, cast expressly for the chapel by Meneely Bell Company, of Troy, New York. The new bell which "has a pleasant tone" bore the inscription: "Union Chapel Association, Falmouth Heights, Mass., 1906. P.D. Cowan, president, A.C.Munroe, Sec-Treas, One Lord, One Faith, One Baptism."[10]

Though the popularity of the chapel continued into the early 1920s, concern was expressed at a meeting of the trustees in 1912, when the death of Mr. Munroe was noted as the loss of a fourth big supporter in a year. Then when only four trustees attended a 1914 meeting, "additional men were voted to serve on the board."[11] A trustee meeting in 1920 discussed improvements to the chapel, but an *Enterprise* article five years later (July 1925) describes an important public meeting where "a number of residents of Falmouth Heights . . . are interested in removal of the observation tower and chapel which has become an eyesore and a menace to the property in the immediate neighborhood." The property is described as "sadly neglected . . . becoming each year more and more dilapidated."[12]

Another *Enterprise* article[13] reported that on Christmas Day 1928, "boys broke practically all the glass in the 29 windows" of the chapel. Then in January 1929, we read that the "observatory has stood vacant for many years . . .is boarded up with paint peeling . . . situated at the intersection of eight streets ascending the hill, it impedes traffic since the introduction of the automobile."[14] By this time the stockholders of the original development company and even their heirs were hard to locate and many of the trustees of the chapel had resigned or died.

The warrant for the Falmouth Town Meeting of February 12, 1929 includes article 63: "To see if the town will vote to request the Selectmen to lay out for highway purposes that portion of land at Falmouth Heights known as the Chapel lot and also known as Observatory Hill, and raise and appropriate the sum of $1000, for the purpose of payment for the land, that being the price agreed to by the Trustees, or set or do anything else in this matter, including taking thereof by eminent domain if deemed advisable or necessary,"[15] The article passed.

A side note for local historians - Town Meeting that year was held at the Elizabeth Theatre, where Maxwell & Co. is now.

In a subsequent meeting with selectmen, C. S. Hannaford, trustee of the old chapel, agreed to the town's taking of the land. He stated that the only other trustee still in office, Mrs. Mabel S. Harris, would concur.[16] Although it had served as a chapel, it was not a consecrated building, so demolition was allowed. By August 1929, the *Enterprise* reported that "Arthur Peterson, contractor, has underway the work of demolishing the old observatory."[17]

Crown Avenue today surrounds a peaceful green where the chapel once stood. Only a few pictures of the demolition are available and none shows the bell. I have been unable to find evidence that the town took inventory of the building contents before the demolition. The current location of the Meneely bell is unknown.

3

THE HOLBROOK BELL
OF LAWRENCE ACADEMY

For the first several years of my searches, the maker of the bell in the cupola atop Lawrence Academy (today the Chamber of Commerce building) was a mystery. I could see the bell from the ground but it was not accessible from inside the building. From outside I tried binoculars and a camera with a telephoto lens. On two occasions I enlisted friends to fly by with their drones (thanks to Tim Kane and Brian Switzer) but the inscriptions could not be read – the lighting and contrast were too much for the drone cameras.

The cupola and bell atop the Falmouth Chamber of Commerce building, originally known as Lawrence Academy. Credit – K. Peal

Eventually I took extreme action and flew up there myself - with help from a Hamilton Tree Company bucket truck (thanks to Dave and Justin). I was able to look at it from all sides and take lots of pictures. These pictures plus subsequent research have convinced me of the importance and also the vulnerability of this historic building. The cupola is particularly fragile – during its lifetime it has already been found rotted or damaged beyond repair several times.[18] My flyby indicated that we are again at a point that we need to take action to avoid losing the cupola. More on that later.

I also had a good look at the bell and determined that it was made in 1835 at the G. H. Holbrook foundry in East Medway, Massachusetts. This agrees with many of the historical documents[19] and confirms that it is the original school bell used at the Lawrence Academy.[20] It is a valuable artifact for the town and identifying it like this adds a formerly unknown Holbrook bell for experts who keep track of such things.[21]

Compared to the cupola, the bell seems robust and indestructible but I learned that during Hurricane Bob (1991) when the whole cupola was blown off the roof, the bell was almost destroyed. Donald Fish kindly showed me his pictures of the cupola in pieces on the ground after the hurricane. They showed that the bell landed on top of the remains of the cupola which probably saved the bell from destruction. A direct landing on the ground would surely have cracked or broken the bell.

The bell called and greeted Lawrence Academy students from its installation in 1835 until 1896 when the school moved to a new building.[22] Academy graduates formed an Alumni Association and at one of the annual meetings (about 1907) a poem 'Lawrence Academy Bell', written by Miss Ellen P. Bates was recited.[23] The poem, running somewhat over 500 words sounds quaint to our ears. Here is a short excerpt:

> *With a front supported by pillars,*
> *And perched on the sloping roof,*
> *A belfry, crowded with birds' nests;*
> *Shelters a bell, whose tones hath spoken to us since childhood.*

Admirers of Katharine Lee Bates may know of her poem "The Falmouth Bell". It refers to the bell at the Congregational Church, not the one at the Academy building.

Here is another tale about the Academy bell. In the exuberance of the Armistice ending the Great War, an *Enterprise* article on Nov 16, 1918 states "the bell on the old Lawrence Academy was rung Monday for the first time in more than twenty years. Most people had probably forgotten that there was a bell in the old belfry, but it didn't take the boys long to discover it. It sounded quite familiar to the old-timers."[24]

But the cupola is the part of the building that we see. A search through *Falmouth Enterprise* articles and Falmouth Historical Society records indicates that the cupola has been through many cycles of renovation and rebuilding, primarily because of its exposure to the elements. My recent bucket truck flyby showed bird droppings everywhere on the bell, the support beam and the roof underneath. The droppings won't permanently damage the bell but they are damaging the roof and can compromise the strength of the beam. Furthermore, the cupola's paint is peeling, the legs are not protected against water damage (there is no flashing) and the roofing material has deteriorated, exposing bare wood. This presents a serious challenge for the town since there is a preservation restriction on the building that includes a "covenant to maintain" clause.[25] The damage to the cupola cannot be seen from the ground so I have been talking about it to the town's new Facilities Manager, Greg Endicott. I hope that the DPW will undertake maintenance to avoid losing the cupola.

Beyond that, here are some things we could do to improve the cupola. In 2016 when CPC funds were used to repair the cupola, that same preservation restriction included this: "Historic views indicate that the cupola retains historic appearance except for the loss of cresting that encircled the square base, pyramidal corner elements, and a simple finial with a weather vane. It is encouraged but not required that these missing elements be reconstructed."[26] Appropriate cresting and corner elements could be made based on old pictures that we have. The weather vane was ready to be installed back in 1975 after George Pimental and a CETA crew had restored it,[27] but for some reason it was never installed. I bet it is in a town workshop somewhere waiting to be found.

It would also be appropriate to get the bell ringing again. During my flyby I performed a simple test to confirm that the bell can still be rung – I hit it with a piece of pipe on a rope (got a video too). At present however, the bell is mounted on a fixed support beam so it can't be rung by swinging. And even though the clapper is still in place, it is resting on the roof and it can't move far enough to ring the bell. A good solution would be to install an electrically powered external striker to ring the bell. This allows the bell to be rung remotely when desired or automatically, perhaps on the hour. That would be the first time for it to ring since the celebration of America's Bicentennial in 1976.[28]

Beyond the historic aspects of the Academy building, its service to a spectrum of Falmouth's citizens is impressive. It was built in 1834 recognizing the importance of educating Falmouth's youth before education was mandated by the state. When the town built its own school in 1896, Town Meeting voted to have the building used by the local post of the Grand Army of the Republic (Civil War).[29] This tradition continued, providing a home for the Sons of Union Veterans, the Women's Relief Corps, the American Legion, and the United Service Organizations (USO).[30] More recently the building housed the Samaritans (suicide prevention) and Neighborhood Falmouth (supporting Falmouth seniors) as well as our Chamber of Commerce.

This building and its bell are treasures that need to be preserved.

4

FOG BELLS WARNED SHIPS
BEFORE HORNS CAME INTO USE

Never heard of fog bells? They came before fog horns. Like fog horns, bells were used in foggy conditions to warn of navigational hazards such as rocky coastlines or shoals. They were installed along with lighthouses on land and on lightships (which serve as lighthouses in water that is too deep for lighthouse construction). Ship's bells were also used to avoid collisions with other ships during fog. Bells were used in the US as early as 1829[31] until it was recognized that the louder, lower frequency sound from fog horns traveled longer distances in foggy conditions than the sound from bells. Fog horns came in to common use about 1900; fog bells served as backups to fog horns for a while but were phased out completely by about 1920. This is a story of three fog bells in Falmouth.

Several years into my retirement I got a call from a young machinist at Woods Hole Oceanographic Institution (WHOI) telling me there was a bell at the WHOI warehouse I should look at. Pulling my emeritus rank I asked for it to be retrieved from its shelf so I could check it out (thanks, Walter Albaugh). What I found was the bell from one of WHOI's famous ships – the RV Chain (RV stands for research vessel, a ship used for research at sea). Originally used to sound alarms and particularly as a fog signal, the bell was one of many prized items saved as memorabilia before the ship was scrapped in 1979. Recently, when I asked Robertson Dinsmore, retired manager of Marine Operations at WHOI about the bell, he said "Oh yes, I was the one who had it stored when Chain was retired to make sure it didn't get lost or stolen but I had totally forgotten about it." He was pleased that we had "found" it again and he hoped we would find a use for it.

Launched as a navy salvage tug in 1943, USS Chain was decommissioned after the war then reclassified for oceanographic research and operated by WHOI starting in 1959.[32] Over the next 20 years the Chain did 129 scientific cruises, perhaps most notable being "Chain-99", the name for the cruise that took her around the world in many legs during 1970-1971.[33] An around-the-world cruise sounds glamorous but in oceanography it means connecting the start and end locations of many disparate experiments to minimize deadheading (when the locations don't quite connect) and yet keep the ship progressing around the world – and eventually back home. There were times during Chain-99 when the ship was far from home and it was not clear how the next leg would be funded. And ship maintenance in foreign ports was always a challenge, especially for this aging ship.

RV Chain entering Woods Hole, showing the bell just above the bridge (round portholes). Credit – Navsource Naval History, US Naval History and Heritage Command

Eventually by 1979 the ship's age intervened and the decision was made to scrap her.[34] Then the ship's fog bell, saved from ignominy, was put on view in one of WHOI's machine shops as a reminder of the beloved ship. But one day it was accidentally struck by a passing forklift causing it to crash to the floor and break into several pieces. Personnel in the shop were able to put humpty dumpty back together but when I found it at the warehouse it gave only a dull thud when we struck it – it is no longer ringable. The shop's repair held the pieces of the bell together but it wasn't resonant. No surprise that it was banished to a far shelf in the warehouse. But, I have suggested to Dutch Wegman, WHOI port engineer, that even though the bell can't be rung it could be put on public display with appropriate signage to commemorate the Chain and the institution's seagoing heritage.

This bell at Bigelow Marine Park was a land-based fog bell that served in the US lighthouse service. The inscription dates it to 1858 or earlier. Credit – K. Peal

You may have noticed the second Falmouth fog bell but not realized it. That is the bell displayed at the Marine Park on Scranton Avenue next to the Harbormaster's Office. It was a land-based fog bell that served in the US lighthouse service. Although it has no date, the inscription, USLHE (United States Light House Establishment), dates it to 1858 or earlier.[35] In later years it would have been marked LHB for the Lighthouse Board, or later still, USLHS when the name was changed to the Lighthouse Service. I have found no good answer to how the bell came to its present location in the Marine Park. Catherine Bumpus told me that the bell was given to the town in the 1960s but we don't know who gave it or where it came from. Another question is if it was ever used at Nobska Point lighthouse in Falmouth. That seems unlikely because records I found for "Nobska

Point Massachusetts" from the United States Lighthouse Society show the use of a fog bell at Nobska identified as LHB rather than USLHE. The records also show that a bell was first used at Nobska in 1878; by then the name Lighthouse Board was in use.[36]

Finally, I found reference to the third Falmouth fog bell in a huge document listing nearly 10,000 bells made by the Meneely bell foundry of Troy, New York.[37] The list was organized by state so I was able to search for Massachusetts and found a 1000 lb. bell that was delivered to "Vessel, Wheeler & Co." in Woods Hole on June 28, 1892. After some sleuthing and again with help from Bob Dinsmore we determined that Wheeler & Co were outfitting a new lightship, LV-54 at the Woods Hole Coast Guard base. According to the website *U.S. Coast Guard Lightship Sailors,* LV-54 was built in 1892 in West Bay City, Michigan, delivered to Woods Hole by the contractor where "alterations were made, it was fitted out and supplied".[38] Among other notes: "FOG SIGNAL ... hand operated 1000 lb. bell". In November 1892 after outfitting, LV-54 went on station to become the lightship on Nantucket New South Shoal. But this is a demanding location; by April 1893 the ship was "off station for repairs", then was "considered unsuitable for such an exposed location". By September 1894 she was withdrawn and reassigned to Boston but that turned out to be no less demanding - she was bumped and even holed more than once by passing ships. She was finally retired in 1946 after 54 years of service. But I bet the Meneely bell was still serviceable.

5

SPOHR GARDENS OFFERS A SPRING ESCAPE AS WELL AS ARTIFACTS

This winter is no different from other winters - we await spring and daffodils. I may be biased but come spring, Spohr Gardens offers the daffodils with the extra bonus of a couple of nice bells.

When the weather improves, head down Woods Hole Road, turn left at Oyster Pond Road then a sharp left onto Fells Road. For those who don't know, the garden is open to the public and run by a private non-profit Trust.[39] Respect the peaceful location and donate funds or gardening expertise if you can. The daffodils are the stars in early spring but the azaleas and rhododendrons will wow you on "Spring at Spohr" day (May 15 this year) and then through the rest of the year you will enjoy the wildflowers, anchors, bollards, millstones, butterflies and bees, all with views of Oyster Pond.

This is where we find perhaps the largest bell in Falmouth – 48" diameter. The Spohr Gardens website says it is 56" diameter but my tape said 48"; still pretty big. It is mounted so that passersby can swing the bell. If you are persistent in swinging it or maybe just grab the clapper and push it against the bell, you will hear a rather clangy sound. Sadly, it has a pretty serious crack. But it is still a treasure and has an interesting, if rather severe inscription.

> SINNERS! The sound of this bell calls you together for the good
> and eternal happiness of your souls and to praise and glorify
> Christ AND ONLY THIS
> This BELL is CONSECRATED to TRUTH presented to the
> Baptist church in East Dedham MASS
> by Jonathan Mann Feb 20 1882

Then the basic fact:

*Cast by William Blake and Co,
formerly H. N. Hooper & Co Boston Mass 1882*

About 2 years ago I had a call from a representative of the Fellowship Bible Church in Dedham, Massachusetts, which I soon discovered occupies the site of the Baptist Church, referenced in the above inscription. Although the original Baptist Church building was demolished in 1970,[40] the Fellowship Bible Church members were planning to celebrate the 175th anniversary of the church which might include retrieving the bell. The Fellowship Church sent several requests to Spohr Gardens about possibly buying back the bell but had received no reply. Of course, I couldn't help them (I still don't know how they got my name) but I was able to trace what happened. Apparently, when the Baptist Church building was being demolished, the bell was given to the demolition company, John J Duane Co., as part payment for the work. Subsequently Charlie Spohr bought the bell from Duane and it is a prized possession.

The other bell at Spohr Gardens is farther down the main path and overlooks Oyster Pond. Little is known about this bell except that it may have come from the "First Catholic Church Patchogue, L.I.". That is the hand-written note on a letter among Charlie Spohr's investigations about the bell when he bought it in 1962.[41] Of course, there is no church by that name in Patchogue but my queries have stirred discussions there among the library, local historians and a couple of parish offices. But no records have been found nor even a parishioner who remembers a bell. So - a dead end.

The markings on the bell "CIN BELL CO" led me to the Cincinnati Bell Foundry Company which took over making bells from Blymyer Manufacturing Company in 1885. Their 1904 catalog, entitled "Those Famous Blymyer Bells" features angels on the front cover with this: "Think when the bells do chime, 'tis angels' music" and has poetry and artwork on alternate pages throughout the catalog. The bell in question appears in the catalog as one of their "Churches, Academies, Court Houses" bells so the bell at Spohr Gardens dates from early in the 20th century. It is a cast steel bell so it is not tuned to a musical note like bronze bells but still it sold for $125 [42] which translates to over $3000 today.

When the snow is really gone, plan a trip to Spohr Gardens to check out the bells – and even enjoy the daffodils.

The larger of the two bells at Spohr Gardens, this one from the Baptist Church in East Dedham, Massachusetts. Credit – K. Peal

Cincinnati Bell Foundry Company's 1904 catalog, titled "Those Famous Blymyer Bells," features angels on the front cover. Credit - From the Collection of Cincinnati & Hamilton County Public Library, used by permission

6

CHURCHES: A REPOSITORY OF HISTORY

A good place to look for historic bells in New England is Congregational churches. Fortunately, we have several in Falmouth. Congregational churches were established as meeting houses for early New England towns, and most of them had bells that were used for communicating with the townsfolk.

The Paul Revere bell at First Congregational Church. Credit – Peter Partridge, used by permission

Many of the meeting houses are well preserved, at least in part because Congregationalism was the established church (supported by taxes) until disestablishment in the early nineteenth century.[43] Today they represent a treasure trove of history.

In Falmouth, the First Congregational Church traces its history to a congregation that gathered in 1708. The building we see today is the fifth meeting house.[44] The Paul Revere bell in the steeple was cast in 1796, documented by the original invoice the church holds for $338.94 signed by Revere. The church website tells us the bell's inscription reads: "'The living to the church I call, and to the grave I summon all", a trademark of Revere Bells. And "that bell continues to ring out over Falmouth".[45]

Several years ago, I arranged for a tour with Jonathan Drury, the current and 29th pastor of First Church. This was before the impressive renovations and maintenance that have recently been completed at the church. The bell is aging well but the fabric of the building requires serious periodic care so the church can retain its historic value and continue serving the community.

The tour started up in the balcony next the organ. Through a door at that level, stairs lead up to the level of the ceiling above the main sanctuary, then on up to the clock and bell level. The Seth Thomas clock mechanism, added in the 1950s, runs the hands on the three faces of the steeple's clock via three separate drive shafts. The clock has a traditional escapement mechanism but is wound electrically. To adjust the clock for daylight saving time (or for any other reason), Jonathan must disconnect all three drive shafts then open a small door in each clock face to reach out to the hands that we see from the street. He can move the hands but can't really see the time, so a helper is needed out on the street to tell him when the hands are set correctly. Once this has been done for all three faces, the three drive shafts must be reconnected before the time changes noticeably. One further complication is that the hourly strike of the bell comes from a separate control system so there is no guarantee that the time of the striker is synchronized with the Seth Thomas clock.

At one point in the tour, Jonathan mentioned that he had heard of another Revere bell in Falmouth but he didn't know where it was. I recently discovered that the North Falmouth Congregational Church might be the basis for that story.

I found another story about the First Congregational bell in an undated booklet in the reference section of Falmouth Library.[46] "It has been said that the leader of the choir tuned his bass viol to the pitch of the bell which was originally C sharp". A slightly different version appeared in an *Enterprise* article [47] "Mr. Landers … used to tune his violincello by the Paul Revere bell the pitch of which was C sharp. When the crack in it came it was and is now C flat". There are several problems with this version. First, I have found no other reference to a crack in the church's bell and it is still intact today. Then, when a bell cracks it often renders the bell unringable since the resonance is destroyed. If the bell was still resonant it is unlikely that its new resonance would be exactly a whole tone lower (C flat, actually B natural, instead of C sharp).

Moving on to Hatchville we find the Second Congregational Church, later known as the East End Meeting House and now the Falmouth Jewish Congregation. It was formed in 1821 by members from Falmouth's First Congregational Church who expressed "considerable dissatisfaction and grievous disappointment in the First Church".[48] The building dates from 1797 but did not have a bell until 1842 when parishioner Shubael Lawrence left money in his estate to upgrade the building and add a bell. So why is the bell currently on the ground rather than in the steeple? It is an interesting story, worth a visit to the Jewish Congregation's website.[49]

In the meantime, you can walk up to the bell on the grounds of the synagogue and see the inscription:

Cast by Henry N Hooper & company
Boston, 1842

You will notice that the bell has a serious crack (so it won't ring) and also that there are four steel spokes connected to the bell. These are the remains of the rope wheel but missing the connecting wooden arches that would guide the rope used to ring the bell. The cause of the crack in the bell is unknown but the loss of the connecting arches due to weathering is not uncommon. In Falmouth we have other bells with a similar wheel design but they are still intact and in use: Woods Hole School and West Falmouth Methodist Church, for example.

Workers from Yankee Steeplejack Co. installed the renovated steeple on Waquoit Congregational Church on a snowy day in February 2010. Credit – Milton Williamson, used by permission

In Waquoit another "second" church, the Second Congregational Meeting House of East Falmouth gathered (in 1847) and occupied the building we see today in 1848.[50] In 1863 the name was changed to Waquoit Congregational Church.[51] The town has watched this beautiful building being restored over the last few years, in part supported by Falmouth's Community Preservation Fund.[52] Unfortunately, we missed an opportunity to learn about the bell while the tower was on the ground during the renovations in 2010 – there are no pictures of the bell. Long after those tower renovations Bob Slater, church archivist, gave me a tour that started with a climb up a ladder from the church balcony into the overhead. To access the bell, so easily seen from outside the church, is a challenge. It requires further climbing up inside the tower, then finding a small door that opens out onto the peak of the roof.

Waquoit Congregational Church tower seen from the bucket truck in October 2020. Credit – K. Peal

From there an inveterate climber - not me - would need to retrieve the small custom-made ladder from inside the tower, reach out with the ladder above his head and hang it onto the edge of the belfry above. Next the climber would crawl out of the tower onto the peak of the roof and climb up the ladder to be faced by the bird screen that has to be removed to gain access to the open part of the tower where the bell is located – whew! That is why, after Bob's helpful tour I made a note to myself: *"Waquoit church bell – not really accessible from inside the building"*.

I made several unsuccessful attempts from outside to read the inscription on the bell: binoculars and telephoto cameras from the ground and drone-based cameras flying up to the bell tower. Finally, I was able to use a bucket truck from Hamilton Tree Co. and get permission from the always-friendly Nell Fields to fly up myself and take a look. Even then the bird screen caused a problem - it confused the digital camera's autofocus algorithm. But close up observation plus a couple of manual focus pictures convinced me that the bell was made by the:

"H. N. Hooper & Company,
Boston Mass, 1850"

    To my knowledge the fact that the bells for both the Waquoit Church and the east End Meeting House came from the Hooper foundry is a coincidence.
    This tour of congregational churches in Falmouth has omitted a surprising story about the North Falmouth Congregational Church and the little-known First Congregational Church of Woods Hole. Stay tuned.

7

A Walking Tour of Woods Hole

Most people know Woods Hole as where you go to get the ferry to the Vineyard or to visit the NOAA aquarium. Lots of people work there in the science labs or the Coast Guard. Others go to a restaurant or an art gallery. Only the locals know about the famous Woods Hole black (it's a type of dog) or Tiny, the bridge tender (everybody's friend). This article will give you a bell tour of the village but during April you can do you own walking tour and participate in Woods Hole Library's scavenger hunt at the same time.

The original 1853 Church of the Messiah, a wooden structure, housed the Hooper bell that was moved to the present granite building when it was consecrated in 1889. Credit – Woods Hole Historical Museum, Woods Hole, MA, used by permission.

As you approach Woods Hole from Falmouth, turn onto Church Street just before Little Harbor and stop at the Church of the Messiah. When

I started asking, there seemed to be no corporate knowledge about the bell in this beautiful granite building although I learned that it is rung regularly. Getting me access to the belfry was smoothed by John Vose who carries a lot of keys on his belt. Carefully climbing up the too-steep ladder we found a 28" Hooper Company (Boston) bell dated 1854. So not only is the name of the foundry now on record but we also know that the bell must have been moved from the former wooden church building, erected in 1853, to the present granite building when it was consecrated in 1889.[53] The original wooden building, moved and recently renovated is still in use as a Parish and Community Center. Before you leave, stroll around the idyllic cemetery that surrounds the church – there are many stories to be told about its famous occupants.

The Woods Hole Congregational Church stood on Main Street, now Water Street. Credit – Woods Hole Historical Museum, Woods Hole, MA, used by permission.

Now, head towards the village and you will see a bell under a shelter located in the courtyard between the library and the Woods Hole Historical Museum. The inscription on the bell tells its story:

McShane Bell Foundry, Baltimore, MD, 1890
The gift of Love H Davis to The First Congregational Church of Woods Holl as a memorial of her husband Jabez Davis of Woods Holl who died April 1ˢᵗ 1889.

(The village was known as "Woods Holl" for a brief period in the late 1800s).

Many people today don't know that there was a Congregational church in Woods Hole. It was located on Water Street beside the current post office. The building, which is now a gift store, lost its tower and belfry to a lightning strike in the 1960s. The congregation had long since ceased to function, and the building was deteriorating. Gloria McLean bought the building in 1966 and generously donated the bell to the Woods Hole Historical Museum.[54] Tom Renshaw built the shelter you see in the library courtyard to protect and display the bell. You can ring it too.

And a modern note, on January 20ᵗʰ this year (2021), a group of villagers happily rang this bell 46 times to celebrate the inauguration of our new president.

Now, turn right onto School Street. On the right is the former Woods Hole Methodist Church which is now the visitor center and museum for the Woods Hole Oceanographic Institution (WHOI). Its bell (Henry McShane, Baltimore, 1884) was moved in 2018 to John Wesley Church in Falmouth and is used regularly there. The visitor center building, then the Methodist Church originally stood on Water Street very close to The Landfall Restaurant. Parishioners of both this church and the Congregational Church opposed Landfall owner Dave Estes's application for an alcohol license. This opposition led Pastor Hollis French, attorney Robert Tilden and selectman Charles Stowers to appear at an appeal before the ABC in Boston in April 1948[55] but the license was granted. That is one reason that the Methodist Church building was moved (in 1949) to its present location on School Street. Another reason is that Dr A. C. Redfield, noted oceanographer and former WHOI assistant director, donated land adjacent to his home for the church to use.[56]

Up over the hill, on the left is the Woods Hole School. Tom Renshaw kindly gave me a tour of this architectural gem, built in 1870, that is on lease from the town and totally maintained by the Woods Hole Community Association. Much of the work is organized by Tom or even done by his own hands. An addition to the school, built in 1885, makes extensive use of treasured "pre-blight" chestnut for door and window casings. The blight was introduced to the US in 1904 with Japanese chestnut trees imported for commercial purposes.[57] This led to the near-total loss of chestnut as a building material.

To access the school's bell, we moved a bookshelf aside then unfolded the hand-built wooden ladder and climbed up to the attic. Carefully navigate around the exposed plumbing up there to another ladder then climb up into the tiny belfry. I found a lovely bronze bell but no inscription. The rope and rope wheel are in good shape. This is the bell that has called kids to the Children's School of Science every summer since 1914.[58] Getting selected to be the kid who pulls the rope (from down below, of course) is still a much sought-after privilege every day of the Science School.

The bell tower at the Mary Garden on Millfield Street. Credit – Catherine Bumpus, used by permission

Next, turn left on Millfield Street, down the hill to the Mary Garden and Bell Tower across the road from St Joseph Chapel, the garden's owner. The two bells in the tower, from the Gillett and Johnston foundry in Croydon, England, dated 1929, are named after giants of the life sciences. The inscription on the larger bell, named for Gregor Mendel is "I will teach you of life – and of life eternal". On the smaller bell, named for Louis Pasteur is "Thanks be to God". Designed to ring the Angelus (7am, noon and 6pm), the bell mechanism initially had to be started by hand every time, then later it was started from a clock across the road in the Rectory. In 1952, retired electrical engineer Wallace Butler designed and installed a system that was completely contained within the tower.[59] It was maintained by Mr. Butler then by Stephen McInnis until Mr. McInnis's death in 1991.[60] In 2010 Matt and Catherine Bumpus did a significant rebuild of the bell works after the mechanism had been neglected for several years. They undertook the work with advice from naval architect, Jonathan Leiby and marine contractor, Dan Clark and against the advice of roof craftsman, Tom Chase - Tom didn't like the look of the ladder inside the tower (neither did Matt). A further upgrade to the mechanism and the tower mentioned in a *Falmouth Enterprise* article[61] was performed by The Verdin Company of Cincinnati, Ohio. The bells sound the Angelus as before but now also ring on the hour and for special occasions.

This little village seems to have all church denominations represented. Notably absent however is the Baptist church. In 1878, a Union Congregation was formed[62] that included Baptist along with Congregational and Methodist churches with plans to share a building and engage clergy alternately from the denominations. Unfortunately, the union split and only the Methodists and Congregationalists were able to continue and build churches in Woods Hole –but even those have now ceased to function.

There are two more bells associated with Woods Hole: the fog bell that came to Woods Hole destined for a lightship – described in chapter 4 – and the bell from the old Woods Hole Fire Station – that story is in chapter 10.

8

THE MYSTERY AT NORTH FALMOUTH CONGREGATIONAL CHURCH

By now readers know of my quest to identify church bells in Falmouth, but trying to unravel the history of the bell at the North Falmouth Congregational Church led to some interesting diversions. The church website[63] mentions that the bell was acquired in 1832 from a church in Sandwich but I couldn't check this because there is no easy way to access the belfry. Fortunately, I got pictures of the bell from Ray Rowitz taken last year when the bell rope in the cupola was being serviced. The pictures clearly showed a bell from the Holbrook foundry, dated 1848. So, now I had two bells to investigate.

The 1848 Holbrook bell, now added to the Chepachet list. Credit – Ray Rowitz, used by permission

First the 1832 bell. The church website offers this: "1832 – North Falmouth meeting house erected … with rounded steeple and Sandwich

Universalists' bell, drayed by Samuel Nye". The verb "dray" is seldom used these days; it means to haul something on a strong cart or a wagon without sides.

I have found two other sources that recount a very similar story: the North Falmouth Church Annual Report from 1972 [64] and *"Churches on Cape Cod"*, a 1974 book by Marion Rawson Vuilleumier.[65] It seems likely that all three stories came from a single earlier source but I have not been able to find that source. But there is a problem with the basic story: there was no Universalist Church in Sandwich until 1845.[66, 67]

This gets a bit confusing. In 1961 the Unitarian Universalist Association (UUA) was formed by consolidating the American Unitarian Association and the Universalist Church of America.[68] The UUA is what we think of today as the "Unitarian church", but until 1961 they were separate, and in Sandwich in 1832 there was a Unitarian Church but no Universalist Church. Maybe the original source for these stories confused the two names and the other writers didn't make the correction. Or, another possibility - maybe the event didn't happen in 1832.

So first, if the bell was retrieved from Sandwich in 1832 it must have come from a Unitarian Church. Although getting the name wrong seems unlikely, I decided to trace the history of Sandwich's First Parish Meeting House, a Unitarian church. The book *"Sandwich, a Cape Cod Town"* by R. A. Lovell traces the history of the meeting house from 1704. Two tantalizing items are mentioned: first, the meeting house "received a Revere bell in 1813"[69]; and second, in 1833 a new building was dedicated on the site of the original meeting house and "it had a new 1500 lb bell".[70] So here is my speculation: the bell from the original meeting house went to the North Falmouth church in 1832 and it was the Revere bell. Is this the "other" Revere bell in Falmouth that First Congregational Church's Jonathan Drury told me about? Lots of speculation but interesting.

Then, the other possibility - the bell did come from a Sandwich Universalist Church but not in 1832. Looking closely, the North Falmouth Church website is the only version of the story that claims the bell was retrieved in 1832; the other two stories don't give a date. In that case the event could have occurred later - when there was a Universalist Church in Sandwich. Unfortunately, without a date it is difficult to find the source of the bell. One way to track it down would be to identify the "Samuel Nye" in the story. That would probably require searching among all the

Nye's in the North Falmouth Church cemetery and elsewhere – more of a diversion than I wanted.

So, the trail of the 1832 bell seems to have gone cold.

The North Falmouth Congregational Church, with modern tower and the 1848 Holbrook bell. Credit – K. Peal

Next, the 1848 bell that we know is now in the North Falmouth Church belfry. The most authoritative list of Holbrook bells, maintained on the website of the Chepachet, Rhode Island Baptist Church[71] shows two bells cast in 1848: one went to East Parish Meeting House in Haverhill, Massachusetts; the other to Union Congregational Church in Greenfield, New Hampshire. No mention of North Falmouth Congregational Church. We know that the inscriptions on both of these bells do not include the name of the church so it is possible that the North Falmouth bell is actually one of these two bells that was installed either in Haverhill or Greenfield then later moved to North Falmouth. To investigate this possibility, I checked the history of these two bells – another diversion.

The Haverhill story is simple and well documented. The bell was installed in the Haverhill Town Hall in 1848 then moved to the Meeting House in 1861. The tower and steeple were restored in 2014; the original Holbrook bell was reinstalled as part of that process and is still there.[72]

The story of Greenfield's Union Congregational Church bell is more complicated. The town of Greenfield built their meeting house in 1795.[73] In 1848 a sanctuary was added to the second floor of the meeting house for the Union Congregational Church but there is no mention of a bell. But I learned from Lenny Cornwell, president of Greenfield Historical Society that their meeting house does have a bell but their records don't show its foundry. After several conversations with me, Lenny asked the present-day town clock winder to examine the bell on his next visit to the tower. This he did and after some serious "dusting" uncovered the Holbrook foundry name along with the expected inscription from 1848. This confirmed the location of the second Holbrook bell and by the way, added important information to the Greenfield Historical Society records.

So now we can say that the North Falmouth Congregational Church bell is a previously unknown Holbrook bell. It has been proudly added to the "Chepachet list". I hope this recognition might encourage present day parishioners of the North Falmouth Church to fill in more of the church's history. Here are some questions. Where did the original "1832" bell come from and what happened to it? Can we identify a likely Samuel Nye from the Nye family history? When was the 1848 Holbrook bell acquired? Was it in place when the steeple blew off the church in the 1938 hurricane as recorded in Mary Lou Smith's *"Book of Falmouth"*?[74] We know that a new spire was installed in 1960,[75] although another source credits Arthur Vidal with that spire[76]; was the Holbrook bell in place then?

9

THE MYSTERY OF THE ROAMING BELL

This is a story about a bell that few living souls have seen, that served two churches that no longer exist and that is now at an unknown location. Trust me, it's still a story.

The first church that the bell served was the East Falmouth Methodist Episcopal Church. The church started in 1852 as an enthusiastic religious society gathering in homes, then later at a school. By 1859 they had organized and built a church – "as pretty a church to preach in as there is in all this region".[77] The building itself was "pretty" and it was adjacent to a peaceful cemetery - the East Falmouth Burying Ground located just off Route 28 near Davisville Road.

The East Falmouth Methodist Episcopal Church where the bell was first used. Credit – John Wesley United Methodist Church archives

Surprisingly it took 38 years for the young church to acquire a bell. It is not known if the delay was due to lack of funding or "finding the appropriate bell" but finally on Sunday morning, January 16, 1898 "the people of this village were very glad to hear the sweet tones of the new bell".[78] The article in the *Falmouth Enterprise* also says that it came from the Blake Bell Co. in Boston but it does not say if it had an inscription that would help us identify it.

The church thrived for many years and even undertook a building renovation in 1906 after nearly 50 years of service.[79] By the 1920's however church attendance was declining, losing members to the larger Methodist church on Main Street in Falmouth (the First Methodist Church of Falmouth). And by 1935 the congregations had merged, with worship services held at the Main Street church.[80] As activity at the East Falmouth building declined, vandalism increased. By 1943 the building had been boarded up for over a year so it was sold, with a provision that the buyer would remove the building from the property.[81] Importantly for this story however, the bell was saved and moved to the church on Main Street before the East Falmouth building was removed.

The Falmouth Methodist Church on Main Street in October 1956. Credit – John Wesley United Methodist Church archives

Following the bell then, our story moves to the church on Main Street which traces its roots farther back, to the first Methodists in Falmouth, a group that gathered in 1809.[82] By 1811 they had built a Meeting House on the Methodist Society Burying Ground (near the Poorhouse and the current Falmouth Police station).[83] That building was moved in 1829 to a lot on the east side of Elm Arch Way at Main Street then replaced in 1848 on the same site with the First Methodist Church of Falmouth, the building we see in old pictures and post cards until the 1950s.[84]

Apparently, this building with its classic New England steeple did not have a bell. In the September, 1921 trustees' minutes, we read: "Voted not to accept the old town bell, as the tower could not be made fit for less than $100".[85] And later, when the bell from the East Falmouth Church became available, there was discussion. November, 1942: "see if the fire department can move the bell from the East Falmouth Methodist Church"[86]; February, 1943: "move the bell and furnace to the cellar of the Methodist Church for $75"[87]; November, 1943: "Mr. A. R. Green to repair the tower for $500".[88] It was installed and went on to serve the church for many years.

I have talked to several current Methodists who remember hearing the bell in their youth, although Cynthia Smith said she remembers it with some trepidation because it seemed to be shaking the whole building. Maybe that was an indication of the condition of the tower or the building. By the 1950s the 100-year-old building was showing its age. It had no indoor plumbing and no foundation; the tower needed more work and the facilities were too small for the growing congregation. Renovation was challenging and expensive so the alternative of building at a new location was undertaken. By late 1955 the church had bought the H. V. Lawrence property on Gifford Street[89] for the new church – to be named John Wesley Methodist Church.[90] And the *New Bedford Standard Times* bought the Main Street property.[91] Later, the *Standard Times* had the Main Street church demolished as planned[92] but not before various items were saved from the church, including the bell.[93]

So, again the bell was removed from a church that was closing. The plan was to use it at the new John Wesley Church. The story of the construction of this new church is replete with funding challenges; eventually the building was completed but the steeple was eliminated from the plan to limit costs. The bell had already been moved to the John Wesley church property on Gifford Street but it became clear that it would not be used there. Jim Cardoza tells me he remembers seeing the bell in a shed on the property but his memory from over 60 years ago has no details that would help us identify it. The shed is now gone, but here the situation gets fuzzy: where did the bell go? I have heard various stories; the two most common are that it was donated to a Methodist church in the western part of Massachusetts or to the East End Meeting House (formerly a Congregational Church but now the Falmouth Jewish Congregation synagogue).

There are a lot of Methodist churches in "the western part of Massachusetts" and the trustees' minutes are silent about any such donation. I have contacted some of the churches directly and also approached several District Superintendents without success. It may be out there but I don't know where.

Following up on the other story – the East End Meeting House - led me to a surprising discovery. In conversation with Cynthia Smith who was office manager of the Falmouth Jewish Congregation for many years, I learned of a bell that was found and retrieved from the former parsonage of the East End Meeting House before the parsonage was sold in 1999 by the Jewish Congregation. Just to be clear, this is not the bell that we see on the lawn in front of the Meeting House but a previously unknown bell that had been stored in the barn of the former parsonage. Rabbi Elias Liberman kindly led me to this new bell, now on the ground near a garden shed beside the Jewish Congregation's office building. My bell mentor, Carl Zimmerman, confidently states that "it is a Blake bell from the 1890s".[94] That takes us full circle to the Blake bell mentioned in the *Enterprise* article from January 1898 about the East Falmouth Methodist Episcopal Church. Could it be the same bell? Was this the third time it was saved? Unfortunately, this bell has no inscription (or it may have been removed) so we can't make a definitive identification and the reality is we don't know if this is the roaming bell.

If anybody has more information or another story, I would be eager to hear it.

10

SOUNDING THE ALARM
IN THE EARLY YEARS OF FIREFIGHTING

Now that I am known for bell hunting, I often get suggestions from friends. Henry Brown told me about a bell he had seen at the East Falmouth Fire station that he thought I should check out. I resisted for quite a while – after all, that's not a church bell, I have to draw a line somewhere, but then there were fog bells, school bells ...

Eventually I couldn't resist so I went and talked to John Rose, chief mechanic at the fire station. In fact, he has two bells and a collection of firefighting memorabilia as well. The main treasure is a 22 ½" diameter bell, inscribed "Cast by Henry N Hooper & Company, Boston 1855" complete with clapper. Where does it fit in to Falmouth's firefighting history? I soon discovered Gordon Todd's 1993 *Spritsail* article[95] about the history of fires and firefighting in Falmouth. It presents a sweeping tale from the ad hoc efforts by neighbors using bucket brigades in the early 1800s and before, through to the Beebe Woods fire in 1947 that could have engulfed the whole town. It is a detailed and dramatic story available online – a great read.

In the early days homeowners and farmers used any way they could to raise an alarm and get help fighting a fire. Initially church bells were used but there were still difficulties. An Oct 1897 article in the *Falmouth Enterprise*[96] tells of a visiting pastor who was the first one at a fire near the Congregational Church. He tried to ring the church's Paul Revere bell but couldn't locate the bell rope. Another story[97] tells of a rubbish fire in East Falmouth that "got away and ran rapidly for the woods nearby. The church bell was rung". In May 1900 in Woods Hole "a key box and key have been placed on the Congregational Church so that a bell may be rung as an alarm in case of fire".[98] In May 1902 an article describes a fire alarm box at the West Falmouth Methodist church. "Break the glass in the front of the box and key will open the East door. Ring bell continuously 5 minutes".[99]

In the late 1800s unofficial groups of men (and some boys) organized to fight fires and eventually they had "hose houses"[100] where they kept the hoses, reels and wagons used during a run to a fire. Often, they actually ran to a fire dragging the wagons by hand over gravel roads. Other times a nearby neighbor would offer his horses. These groups and their equipment became the core of the department when town meeting eventually agreed in 1897 that a fire department should be formed,[101] although the chief's salary was $2.00 per year for many years.[102] These stations used various means to sound an alarm when a fire was detected – like the Hooper bell that John Rose has at the East Falmouth Station. Several clues indicate that his bell came from the Woods Hole station - that is, the old fire station on Water Street next to the Community Hall (they called it Liberty Hall[103]), not the new one across the bridge. Here are the clues: Gordon Todd mentions it in passing in the *Spritsail* article; Charlie Clarkin, retired fire fighter and deputy Chief, remembers ringing it at the Woods Hole Station early in his career (1958); and Catherine Bumpus recently sent me a picture of the inside of the hose tower that shows a bolt pattern on the beam where the bell was mounted that matches the hole pattern on top of the Hooper bell. The bell had been fixed to the beam and was run by pulling the clapper rather than swinging the bell. Pulling the clapper makes the bell ring much more rapidly than swing it does, thus producing a truly "alarming" sound.

The bell's date, 1855, makes it much older than Woods Hole Station but I am assured that it was probably bought as a used bell especially since it has those holes exposed on the top instead of a yoke or headstock that would have been provided by Hooper for the original owner.

In trying to date the Woods Hole station, I got a document[104] from the Woods Hole Historical Museum Archives that was a transcription of a "conversation" sponsored by the Woods Hole Library's Historical Committee in 1977 entitled History of the Woods Hole Fire Station. It was a discussion with James Gifford and Sumner Hilton sharing their reminiscences – we are lucky to have access to that historic evening. Among other stories is one about the building.[105] It was moved to its present location in 1912 but in 1919 a new truck – a "Maxim Combination Chemical" – was assigned to Woods Hole that was found to be too big for the building. Undaunted, they physically raised the building inch by inch, using jacks and some 300 ties borrowed from the nearby railroad sheds. When the building was raised 9 or 10 feet in the air they built a new "downstairs" underneath, high enough for the truck. Take a closer look at that building next time you drive by (or when you are in the mob at the start of the Falmouth Road Race). The hose tower where the bell was located was added to the building in 1925.[106]

A 1921 picture of the Woods Hole fire station showing the short-lived porch on the second story. In the foreground is a group of firefighters and dignitaries posing on the new Ford Chemical fire truck. Credit – Original at Woods Hole Fire Station, photographed by K. Peal

The 1993 *Spritsail* article includes this observation about the Woods Hole station after the second story was constructed: "an overhanging porch served as a post for observing passing traffic on Water Street, with many an audible snappy comment hurled back and forth over its railing". Charlie Clarkin's guess is that the porch was removed because the snappy comments got out of hand. Colleen Hurter pointed me to a picture dated 1921, that shows the porch. The focus of the picture is the "Ford Chemical" fire truck but this may be the only picture we have that shows the porch – kind of a treasure.

To learn more about fire bells and fire department history I visited Chief Tim Smith at headquarters. He showed me three commemorative bells as well as a collection of pictures and memorabilia that might be the basis of a firefighting museum. It would be hard to replace what was lost when the New England Fire and History Museum in Brewster closed in 2005[107] but this could still be a deserving project. The bells Tim showed me are highly polished with inscriptions to three former firefighters: Deputy Clifford Amaral who died nearly 30 years ago, call man Reuben F Briggs who died in an accident in 1979 at age 20 and Chief Russell Robbins, who served the department from 1956 to 1986.

The decorative bell in the 9/11 memorial park at Falmouth Fire Rescue Department headquarters. Credit – K. Peal

Finally, Tim showed me the 9/11 memorial in front of the headquarters building right on Main Street – we all drive by there, usually without looking. It's worth a stop (park on King Street or in one of the visitor spots at the fire station) to see this moving display with its massive piece of twisted steel from one of the twin towers and several commemorative items including a decorative bell and a fire helmet mounted on two granite columns that represent the towers. The firefighter's union and volunteer labor made this happen. The bell is rung annually as part of the 9/11 service held there.

11

BELLS AT ST. BARNABAS EPISCOPAL CHURCH

One of my early forays into a church steeple was at St. Barnabas where I learned the architectural challenges they present. It was a rainy December day and not only did I get wet but I could see lots of evidence of repairs aimed at keeping rain out of the lower portion of the tower. Bells are usually mounted up high and open to the air so the sound can travel. But weatherproofing the structure below the bell is difficult especially if you provide a hatch for access to the bell. If the hatch is not completely sealed it is like a roof with a leak. I learned from Tom Chase many years ago that the fastest way to let Mother Nature take over a building is to leave roof problems unrepaired (his sentiment, not his words).

At St. Barnabas, evidence of the damage that can be done by continuous exposure to the elements occurred in 1958 when the warden of the parish, Harry Cocks, made one of his infrequent visits to the belfry to discover that "one of the two heavy wooden supports on which the bell had rested for decades, weakened by long weathering, gave way. The bell rested in precarious balance, the other support also weakened."[108] Ironically the reason for his visit to the tower was to discuss weatherproofing work with a contractor. Recognizing the urgency of the situation, Harry enlisted another contractor, Walter Cockerham, who happened to be working in the rectory at the time. His crew had no experience with bell work but one R. Gilbert Allenby used blocks and tackles to raise the two-ton bell while the Cockerham crew shaped and put in place new supporting beams – probably the same beams that I saw when I visited on that rainy December day. The bell was ready for use again for services the following Sunday.

The bell in the St. Barnabas steeple is inscribed with a trademark "Hooper & Co," which is about 1.5 inches square.
Credit – K. Peal

The bell in the St. Barnabas steeple is from the Blake Foundry in Boston, inscribed as given by James Arthur Beebe in 1891. It also includes a tiny trade mark "Hooper & Co", which at about 1.5 inches is a surprisingly delicate touch. And unusual - it is the only one that I have seen.

The bell's donor, James Arthur Beebe, was the brother of E. Pierson Beebe who founded St. Barnabas parish in 1888.[109] The church website tells us that "the name, St. Barnabas, is attributed to the church having been consecrated on the feast day of St. Barnabas, June 11, 1889".[110]

The new bell was used for the first time at the Ascension Day service in 1891. The ringing of the bell caused the service to be interrupted when volunteer firefighters "gathered from all directions at the church door with anxious inquiries as to where the fire was. The rector gave them a short instruction on the church ecclesiastical calendar, and a very warm welcome to the service inside, but like the invited guests in the parable, they had other previous engagements, and departed somewhat disappointed, he thought, while he turned again to the feeble flock inside". That quote is from a classic tongue-in-cheek letter to the *Falmouth Enterprise*[111] from

Rev Henry Herbert Smythe, second rector of St. Barnabas and president of the Falmouth Historical Society.

Sadly, just over a year later Rev Smythe died suddenly – "was beloved in church and community during 40 years of faithful service". After the moving funeral service "the church bell was tolled seventy-six times, one stroke for each year of life and symbolically as the sexton Joseph MacKilligan gave the final stroke the rope snapped and fell coiled about his feet".[112]

A second bell at St. Barnabas is found atop the Chapel that overlooks Siders Pond. The chapel which was converted in 1962 from the 1894 Carriage Sheds was the gift of William Peters.[113]

Workers install the Lawrence School Meneely bell in the tower of the St. Barnabas Chapel in 1962. Credit - This picture is from Woods Hole Historical collection's *Spritsail*, v. 3, n.1, 1989, by the Rev. T.E. Adams Jr., "Mr. Beebe Has Got His Parish."

The southeast side of the chapel is all windows providing a view of the pond. The other three walls are cut stone untouched from the old Carriage Sheds. In addition to creating the chapel, Mr. Peters wanted the chapel to include a bell tower and a bell. His tower incorporated matching hand-cut stone provided by the Baker Monument Company but Mr. Peters had some difficulty finding an appropriate bell, rejecting locomotive and other smaller bells. Fortuitously a friend, Frederick Lawrence "suggested the old high school bell".[114] I don't know how Mr. Lawrence knew about the school bell or why it seemed appropriate to be used on a church chapel. But at their next meeting "the School Committee gave permission to loan the bell to the chapel" and it's there today. At nearly 60 years so far, I guess it was a long-term loan.

The picture from 1962 shows the bell being installed without mechanical aids by three local workers, only one of whom is known at this point - Henry Brown (on the right), father of my friend of the same name. Captions for this picture typically refer to this as a "400 lb bell". But in fact, it is a 309 lb Meneely bell from Troy NY.[115] The bell is inscribed "Lawrence High School, 1895."

An explanation of exactly which Lawrence School the bell came from (the name Lawrence has been used on at least three schools in Falmouth) and where it was found (not in any of the Lawrence Schools) are stories for another day.

12

THE LAWRENCE HIGH SCHOOL BELL AT ST. BARNABAS CHURCH

In a previous chapter about the bells at St. Barnabas church, we found that one of the bells was from the Meneely Bell Company and was inscribed "Lawrence High School 1895". We know that it was loaned to St. Barnabas by the school committee in 1962 but the next task is to identify which school it came from. The only building that still exists with that name is Lawrence School on Lakeview Avenue. It was built in 1953[116] and never had a bell. And although it was originally named Lawrence High School, now it is a middle school and for that reason it is customarily referred to as Lawrence School.

No, we are looking for an older building. Readers may remember that the current Chamber of Commerce building (built in 1834) was formerly called Lawrence Academy and that the name was changed to Lawrence High School after the town bought the building in 1891. This building does have a bell but it is still in the cupola and besides it is dated 1835 and inscribed G. H. H. for its maker George H. Holbrook. So, that is the wrong building and the wrong bell.

This is where it gets confusing. Shortly after purchasing Lawrence Academy, overcrowding led the town to decide to replace it with a new school that was built just east of our current library (but long before the library was there and before either Katharine Lee Bates Road or Shore Street extension were there). Part of the decision was to "move" the school to the new building but retain the name – so a third Lawrence High School. This school was built in 1895[117] and the town annual report for that year shows the purchase of a Meneely bell for $85.42[118] so probably that is the bell that went to St. Barnabas.

The handsome shingle style Lawrence High School of 1895, was considered a model of its type and was published in several educational journals. The name was retained after this building was demolished in 1954 and the high school moved to the building on Lakeview Avenue. Credit – courtesy of Falmouth Historical Society, Falmouth, MA

But not so fast. Look at the picture of the 1895 Lawrence High School – do you see a bell or even a belfry anywhere? I have looked at pictures of the building taken from all angles and I don't. But there was a bell: a *Falmouth Enterprise* article in June 1931 tells of ringing the school bell to celebrate the baseball team – we defeated Middleboro in the last game topping a near perfect season: 13 and 1.[119] Then on a more momentous occasion, the school bell was rung Oct 24, 1950 at noon along with many bells throughout Falmouth and elsewhere in the country to commemorate the 5th anniversary of the United Nations charter coming into force.[120]

Surprisingly by 1954 the building was ready for demolition as reported in a March 19 *Enterprise* article,[121] headlined "Abandoned to Memories, Old High School Waits in Dust and Debris for Wreckers". Paintings and old desks that will be lost are pictured as are busts of Lincoln and Washington that will be rescued. An accompanying article is headlined "Colorful Stories of Older School days are recalled". Pretty extensive coverage but there is no mention of the school's Meneely bell.

The school, named after Henry W. Hall, its first principal, was Falmouth's first junior high school. The building was torn down in 2003 but the cupola from the building was saved and now stands in a garden on the southwest corner of the school property. Credit – Falmouth Public Library, Anita Gunning post card collection, Creative Commons

Fast forward to May 1962 we learn from an *Enterprise* article "big bell from old Lawrence High School dug out from a pile of books in the Hall School basement".[122] Some readers may never have heard of the Hall School. Before the present Mullen-Hall school there were two schools on the same property: Mullen and Hall. The Hall school, built in 1925, was our first venture into a junior high system and also the first large masonry school building in Falmouth.[123] It was located near the eastern edge of the property facing west, about where Hamblin Avenue is now. In fact, the town had a nice, green campus with the Lawrence High, Mullen and Hall schools and the Memorial Library (built in 1901) all surrounding playing fields and adjacent to Shivericks Pond.

So, why was there a "pile of books" in the basement? That probably relates to roof leaks and structural problems that developed at the Hall school – in November 1959 an inspector declared that some basement rooms could not be used.[124] Then in September 1960, just at the start of the school year an inspector closed the school.[125] A stressed school committee found solutions to the problems and the town continued to use the school for many years. It is quite likely that the bell was uncovered as a result of some of the fairly serious maintenance and renovations that were carried out to allow the school to continue operating. Ultimately the building was torn down in 2003[126] and the expanded Mullen School was renamed Mullen-Hall.

But there are still questions. Where was the bell located in the old Lawrence High School building? How was it saved from the wrecker's ball in 1954? Why was it moved to the Hall school basement? Moving a 300 lb bell through hallways and up and down stairs would not be undertaken lightly. Retired teacher Harry Thomas tells me he certainly remembers the clutter in the basement of the Hall school but he wasn't the one who found the bell. Who did find it?

A final note about naming school buildings. *The Book of Falmouth*[127] tells us "In accordance with a resolution passed at the 1972 Annual Town Meeting [the new high school] was named Falmouth High School. The Lawrence High School name was now a part of history."

13

THE PAUL REVERE BELL
OF THE CONGREGATIONAL CHURCH

I was recently involved in the celebration at First Congregational Church of the town's only Paul Revere bell. The event, called Paul Revere Day, was led by Greg Mills to celebrate the bell's 225th anniversary but it was really an opportunity to look again at the importance of the bell to the town and the church. Greg and the group he formed created an interesting event. The group included Reverend Jonathan Drury, Olivia White from the Falmouth Historical Society and Jeannine Jeffrey, the church's archivist. Documents from the event have been added to the long history of the bell. My investigations unearthed a few new gems about the bell but mostly I learned what others had previously uncovered and I gained new insights about the bell and the history it has seen.

First Congregational Church steeple. The Paul Revere bell is in the louvered portion above the Seth Thomas clock. Credit – K. Peal

The Paul Revere Bell

Paul Revere, the man, is known first for his patriotic activities in the early days of our country but also for his many careers: silversmith, dentist, engraver, printer. He ran an iron foundry, a powder mill (gun powder of course, not cosmetics), a copper rolling mill and a bell foundry. The bell foundry that he started in 1792, when he was 57 years old, became famous for the quality of its bells and because his was the first American foundry to make more than a few bells. We have several documents he made called inventories or "stock lists". He made them for a variety of reasons, so modern interpretations of them differ - I have seen claims that his foundries made several hundred[128] to over 900 bells.[129] One of the largest bells and his personal favorite was sold to King's Chapel in Boston in 1816 – "the sweetest bell we ever made".[130] He died less than a year later but fittingly, that same bell was rung to mark his passing.[131]

Paul Revere and his bells have been studied by many historians. An early one was Arthur H Nichols, a physician from Boston who published books about Revere's bells in 1904 and 1911,[132] but these studies were clearly a sideline. More committed were Ed and Evelyn Stickney, a couple from Bedford, Massachusetts who spent over 30 years personally visiting every Revere bell they could locate. Based on these travels they published definitive books describing the bells.[133] They visited the bell here in Falmouth on at least two occasions (the first time in 1953).[134] My own efforts involved a visit to the Paul Revere House in Boston's North End, and online consultations with staff at the Bedford Historical Society, and the Massachusetts Historical Society, all of which have significant holdings about Paul Revere.

Some letters of the bell's inscription that are deteriorating. The full inscription is "The living to the church I call and to the grave I summon all". Credit – K. Peal

Although ours is certainly a Revere bell, the inscription does not include the word "Revere". In 1986, parishioner Jack Allen invited Ed Stickney to visit again, and they found faint evidence of "Revere", "Boston" and "1796" on the bell but located away from the main inscription. After the visit, Ed Stickney said, "This now proves without a doubt it is an original Revere bell".[135] Why have these three words almost disappeared? I recently took some closeup pictures of the main inscription and showed them to renowned bell expert, Carl Zimmerman, pointing out that some of those letters too have fallen off or are disintegrating, leaving almost no evidence on the bell of where they were. His reply was that the inscription on this bell was formed with letters that were somehow applied to the bell after it was cast. Normally a bell's inscription is built into the mold, so the letters are part of the bell material rather than being made up of visibly applied letters. Carl's comment was "It seems there's no end to the new things we continue to learn about bells!" There is no explanation as to why the inscription on this bell was made that way, but it does explain why a portion of it has disappeared.

As well as the bell itself, we have the original invoice for the bell signed by Paul Revere. The church has a copy on display. The original is normally safely stored away by the Falmouth Historical Society, but it was on display at our Paul Revere Day celebration. Records indicate that back in 1900 the receipt was presented to the Society by Martha Butler, a life-long Falmouth resident.[136] We don't know where it was from 1796 to then (over 100 years!) but fortunately Martha found it in her family papers and recognized its value. Curious about Martha, I found that she has a connection with another historical Falmouth institution – Lawrence Academy, the building now occupied by the Chamber of Commerce. Lawrence Academy was built in 1834 to provide what we now call high school education before it was commonly available or required by the state of Massachusetts. Martha was a member of one of the first classes to attend Lawrence Academy in about 1841. An article in the *Falmouth Enterprise*[137] describes an "Exhibition at Lawrence Academy" that took place in 1844 that included hymns, orations, declamations, compositions, etc. – sounds like an early version of a parent's night. Martha and her sister, Abigail, were among the performers. Then in her later years she did us all an important service by saving the invoice from oblivion.

It is difficult to get a historical perspective when we talk about a bell from 1796. Maybe this will help. In 1865 the Civil War ended, and Lincoln was assassinated; that was 69 years AFTER our bell was cast. And by the end of the First World War, the bell was 122 years old. The bell has marked many other important events over the years. It rings for worship services, weddings, and funerals; the old Seth Thomas clock in the steeple makes sure it also rings on the hour throughout the day. And lest we take it for granted, the only Revere bell older than ours that is still in use is the 1795 bell in the Groveland Congregational Church (Groveland, Massachusetts).[138] Yes, ours is the second oldest Paul Revere bell still in continuous operation.

14

THE EAST FALMOUTH SCHOOL BELL
WHERE IS IT?

Remember the bell at the East Falmouth School? Maybe not, it has been gone for nearly 40 years. It was in a fixed display outside the building on a small platform in the courtyard to the right of the school as you look at it from Davisville Road. It was installed there by Ray Kenney in 1967 when he became principal.[139] He found it among some junk in the basement of the school and realized its historic importance - it had been used in two former schoolhouses in East Falmouth.

The missing bell as it was seen outside the school in this 1967 photo. Credit – *The Falmouth Enterprise,* used by permission

My friend Lynne Brown, who worked at the school for many years, remembers the bell and was the one who got me started. I have searched various sources and talked to many people who might know about the bell. Here is what I have discovered.

The East Falmouth Schoolhouse constructed in 1866 as part of the consolidation plan replacing the former 19 districts each with individual village schools. This is where the bell was first used. Credit – from the collection of Mike Crew, source unknown, used by permission

It was originally used in East Falmouth's traditional one-room schoolhouse that was built in 1866.[140] This was one of the new schools built when the town changed from having 19 school districts, each with its own village school to a consolidated system with fewer districts and buildings. The school stood on the state highway directly across from the East Falmouth Methodist church and its historic cemetery, together forming the center of East Falmouth. The school served until about 1923 when it was replaced by a newer school.[141] The building survived however, and was sold to a private owner with the proceeds of the sale going towards building the new schoolhouse.[142] The original school building still stands (without its belfry) as a private residence, outliving the church building that was removed in 1943. The cemetery is still there.

The "Corner School" built in 1922 at the intersection of Davisville Road and East Falmouth Highway about where the CVS store is now. The bell, moved from the original 1866 schoolhouse, was in the cupola on the right. Credit – Public record, Falmouth Public Schools

The new school was a white clapboard one-story building built in 1922, located about where the CVS store is now. Howard Barrows, long-time Falmouth educator and principal, referred to this building as the Corner School because of its location at the intersection of the highway and Davisville Road. Joe Netto told me he remembers ringing a bell when he was a student there. We can't be sure but probably it came from the 1866 school. Joe told me lots of other stories about his time at that school too - ask him about it some time. There were problems with the building, outlined in a 1956 article in the *Enterprise* "Case for a New School".[143] There were heating issues (the school had to be closed on more than one occasion during cold weather), the walls were thin, there was no gym, the classrooms were small and there was no provision for food preparation.

The "New School" in the *Enterprise* article of course is the one we now see on Davisville Road. Howard Barrows was the principal of this school when it was first occupied in 1958. At a celebration in Howard's honor in 1965, the playground at the school was designated "Howard F. Barrows playground" recognizing it "as the school he helped create".[144] The bell from the Corner School was installed on a brick platform in the school courtyard. But today the bell and platform are gone and the courtyard has an outline map of the USA on the ground, organized years ago by teacher Harry Thomas. Harry remembers the bell that was there before the map; he estimates that the bell was 18 inches across. Mary Lou Botelho, my connection to a group of retired Falmouth teachers (including Lynne Brown) reports that some in the group remember the bell but no one seems to know what happened to it. At least for now, it is missing.

In addition to the three schools where the bell was used there was an earlier (1838) schoolhouse further down Davisville Road.[145] It may have had a bell[146] but more importantly it was part of benevolent efforts begun in 1821 by a few local residents to bring education to Davisville which in those days was viewed as separate from East Falmouth. It continued providing education until the students moved to Falmouth's Corner School when it was occupied in 1922. The story is nicely told in the *Book of Falmouth*[147] noting with pride that the residents' independent educational undertaking had lasted "more than 100 years". The schoolhouse was sold in 1927[148] and became a private residence which still stands, much altered and moved back from Davisville Road.

Historically, eighteenth century schools were in private homes or in small village schools that did not have bells. Later and through the 19th century bells became an important element of most schools in part demonstrating the importance we place on education. They were used to start and end each school day and to announce class changes during the day. But then by the early 20th century, bells were being replaced by electric bells or gongs and eventually by synchronized electric clocks with buzzers or electric bells. An *Enterprise* article in 1932[149] describes such a clock as one of the exciting features of the new Mullen school. But it also portended the end of traditional school bells.

The missing East Falmouth bell is of interest because there are only three other school bells remaining in Falmouth. Together these four cover much of the period when school bells were in use. The oldest of the four, 1840, came from the North Falmouth School and is safely stored at the Falmouth Historical Society. Then the missing East Falmouth School bell, probably cast in 1866. The Woods Hole School bell cast about 1870 is still in use mostly during the Children's School of Science. Finally the bell from the Lawrence High School cast in 1895 is in use at the chapel of St. Barnabas Church.

The question is - does anyone know what happened to the East Falmouth school bell? My best guess is that it was removed along with its platform in about 1980 during construction of the new wing at the school but someone out there may know better. In trying to find where it is now, I have talked to teachers, custodians, students, administrators, superintendents, DPW personnel, librarians, and historians but maybe I missed you. I hope this article may trigger a memory that will help solve the mystery.

15

Bell History and Technology

The bells elsewhere in this book are of interest because of the history they represent and the stories they tell. This chapter aims to give basic, factual information about the broader world of bells: their variety, how they are made, who makes them and how they work. It is an introduction for the more curious reader but certainly not required reading.

This is not a bell primer, just some interesting things I learned while reading about historic bells. Other people have more expertise than I do; some of them are mentioned in the acknowledgments that follow.

Bells and their Uses

A tower bell is hung in the tower of a church or school so the sound can be heard from afar. Other types of bells are found at factories, farms, court houses, fire stations, light houses; on ships, locomotives, fire engines; and in clock towers. The word bell is also used for everything from jingle bells to the chimes used in a symphony orchestra.

A church bell is used as a call-to-worship or to announce a wedding or funeral. Other bells are meant to issue a warning (for a fire or fog or navigation) or to mark the hours.

Bells are made in sizes from hand held to several feet in diameter. Large bells weigh thousands of pounds.

BELL HISTORY AND TECHNOLOGY

HOW BELLS ARE RUNG

For the historic bell in the picture, the ringing sound is made either by the clapper (D) or the toller (F) striking near the rim of the bell. To use the clapper, a rope wraps around the wheel (H) and runs down to a lower room of the tower where it can be pulled to cause the bell to rotate on the bearings (R) until the clapper strikes the bell. The other way to ring this bell uses a rope on the toller that is pulled causing it to strike the bell – in that case, the bell doesn't move. A toller can also be activated by an electrical drive mechanism instead of using a rope.

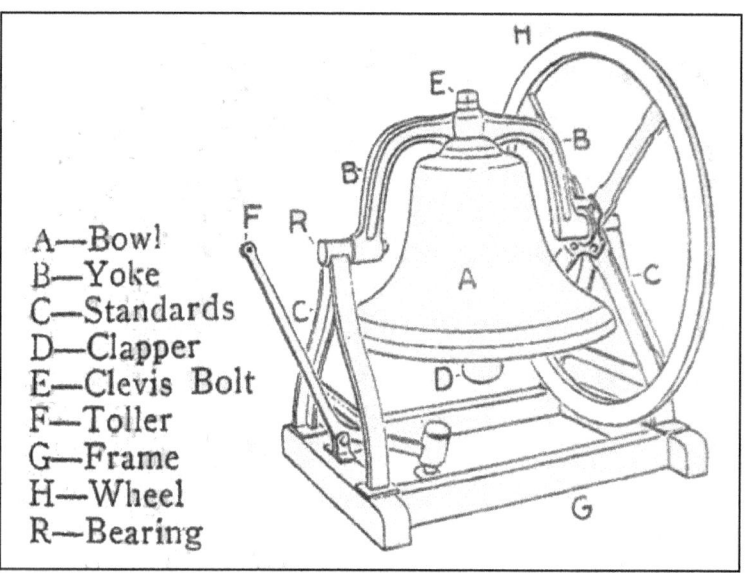

A—Bowl
B—Yoke
C—Standards
D—Clapper
E—Clevis Bolt
F—Toller
G—Frame
H—Wheel
R—Bearing

Sometimes bells are rung by pulling a rope connected to the clapper or by just striking the bell with a heavy object. Hand bells are rung by moving your hand and wrist to make the clapper impact the bell.

Some installations include more than one bell. A group of two or more swinging bells is called a peal. A group of up to 22 stationary bells is called a chime. These are tuned to notes on the musical scale and are rung to play recognizable sequences such as Westminster chimes. In England a time-honored hobby consists of ringing bells in complex, varying sequences called changes. Each participant rings one bell and must synchronize each of his rings to follow the changing sequence being performed. Depending

Bells from many American foundries are found in Falmouth: Revere, Holbrook, McShane, Blake, Meneely, Cincinnati and Hooper. At one location however, the bell tower in the Mary Garden of St Joseph's Church in Woods Hole, we find two bells from Gillett and Johnston, a foundry in Croydon, England.

A more complete list of historic foundry names would include Troy, C S Bell, Richardson, Stuckstede, Blymyer, Buckeye, Cincinnati and Ohio. The actual company names are often some combination of names we know but in a different sequence. Here is one sequence of company names: Paul Revere; Revere & Sons; Revere & Son; Paul Revere & Son; Revere & Blake; Paul Revere & Company; and Revere Copper Company. This may be an indication of how competitive and challenging the business was.

INSCRIPTIONS

An inscription is the lettering seen on the outside of a bell. It usually comprises the foundry name and the casting date. Inscriptions also frequently include information about the purchaser or donor who paid for the bell. Bells that have no inscription were probably made to be held in stock for future sale rather than to fill a specific order.

Inscriptions that go beyond the foundry name and date can include wording specified by the purchaser. These vary from simple memorials or dedications to quite long poetic or pithy sayings.

America's Liberty Bell includes a biblical quote from Leviticus: "Proclaim liberty throughout all the land unto all the inhabitants thereof". Revere bells often use: "The living to the church I call, and to the grave I summon all". This is a variation of "I to the church the living call, and to the grave do summon all" which has been used on English bells since the 1500s.

BELLS AS HISTORY

The story of bells and bell foundries has drawn the attention of historians. Paul Revere has his own museum, in Boston's back bay (about more than just his bells, of course). Edward and Evelyn Stickney, now both passed, were the country's leading experts on Revere bells.

Organizations such as the American Bell Association have an active membership with regular meetings and publications. They are "a network of bell collectors, enthusiasts, researchers, bell ringers, carillonneurs, artisans, manufacturers, technicians and dealers".

Other groups have recreated the history and inventory of several notable foundries. For example, a small church in Chepachet, Rhode Island got interested in Holbrook bells because they had one in their belfry. They now maintain an official list of Holbrook bells – the Chepachet List – documenting dates and locations of many extant Holbrook bells. My investigations inadvertently discovered a new one (at the North Falmouth Congregational Church) which has been added to the list.

Another area of historic interest is construction details used by various foundries. These details include the shape of the body of the bell, the type of crown or clevis pin used, the number, location and style of the reeds (decorative raised ridges around the bell) and the presence or absence of the bell's weight or trade marks stamped on the surface. Using these features, experts can often identify a bell's foundry and approximate casting date even if it has no inscription.

16

MAPS AND FACTS

This section shows the location and technical details of the bells that appear in this book (there are more). The four maps were made by carefully unfolding the "Street and Highway Map of Falmouth, 1934" (cover shown), which is held by the Falmouth Historical Society.

Each numbered black symbol on a map represents one of the bells. The same number appears in the "Map Ref" column of the table where more information about that bell is found. A white symbol is used for bells that are missing.

The "Chapter Index" column of the tables lists the chapter numbers in the book where each bell is mentioned.

Data about the bell's weight, size and casting date are from actual measurements or published material or markings on the bell (including its inscription). When these are not available, values in the table are shown in parentheses to indicate that estimated values were used instead.

MAPS AND FACTS

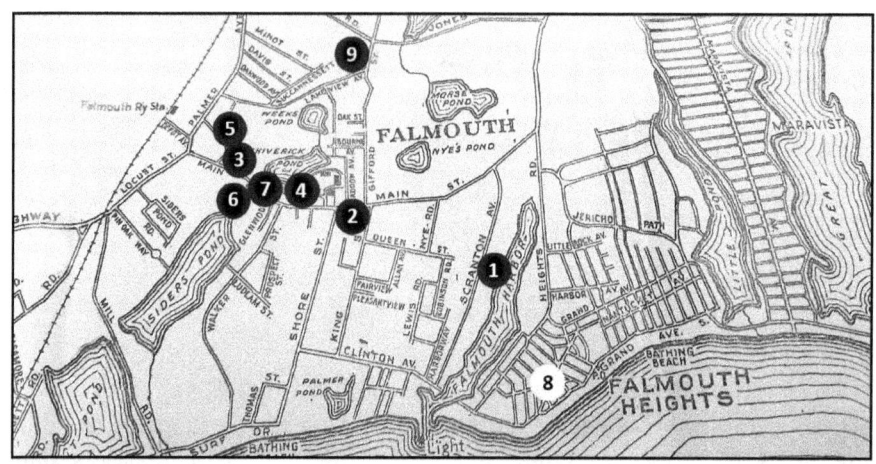

DOWNTOWN

Name of Bell	Location	Map Ref	Chapter Index	Foundry	Type	Dia in	Wgt lbs	Date
Falmouth Marine Park	Falmouth Marine Park	1	1,4	(USLHE)	Coast Guard	33		(1850)
Fire Dept 9/11	Fire Dept garden	2	10	(unknown)	commem-orative	10		(2003)
Fire Dept Amaral	Fire Dept rotunda	2	10	(unknown)	fire engine	12		
Fire Dept Robbins	Fire Dept rotunda	2	10	(unknown)	fire engine	12		
Fire Dept Briggs	Fire Dept rotunda	2	10	(unknown)	fire engine	12		
First Congregational	First Congre-gational	3	1,3,6,8, 10,13	Revere	church	32	807	1796
Lawrence Academy	Lawrence Academy	4	1,3,13	Holbrook	school	(24)	350	1835
North Falmouth School	Falmouth Historical Society	5	14	Blake	school	18	(125)	1840
St. Barnabas garden	St. Barnabas garden	6	11,12, 14	Meneely, Troy, NY	school	(18)	309	1895
St. Barnabas tower	St. Barnabas tower	7	1,11	Blake	church	37	(1000)	1891
Union Chapel	(missing)	8	2	Meneely Troy, NY	church		212	1906
Woods Hole Methodist	John Wesley Church	9	1,7	McShane	church	27	(400)	1884

72

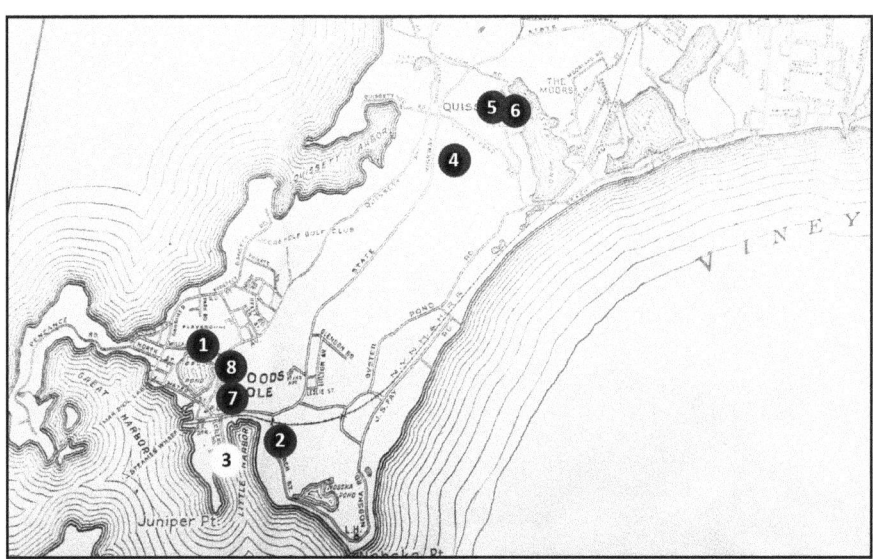

Woods Hole

Name of Bell	Location	Map Ref	Chapter Index	Foundry	Type	Dia in	Wgt lbs	Date
Bell tower, Mendel	Bell tower	1	1,7	Gillett and Johnston	church			1929
Bell tower, Pasteur	Bell tower	1	1,7	Gillett and Johnston	church			1929
Church of the Messiah	Church of the Messiah	2	7	Hooper	church	28	(450)	1854
Lightship	(missing)	3	4,7	Meneely, Troy, NY	ship		1006	1892
RV Chain	WHOI warehouse	4	4	(navy)	ship	22	180	1944
Spohr Gardens, bronze	Spohr Gardens	5	1,5	Blake/ Hooper	church	46	2106	1882
Spohr Gardens, steel	Spohr Gardens	6	1,5	Cincinnati	(unknown)	36	(550)	(1910)
Woods Hole Congregational	Woods Hole Museum	7	6,7	McShane	church	30	642	1890
Woods Hole School	Woods Hole School	8	1,6,7,14	(unknown)	school	21	(200)	(1885)

MAPS AND FACTS

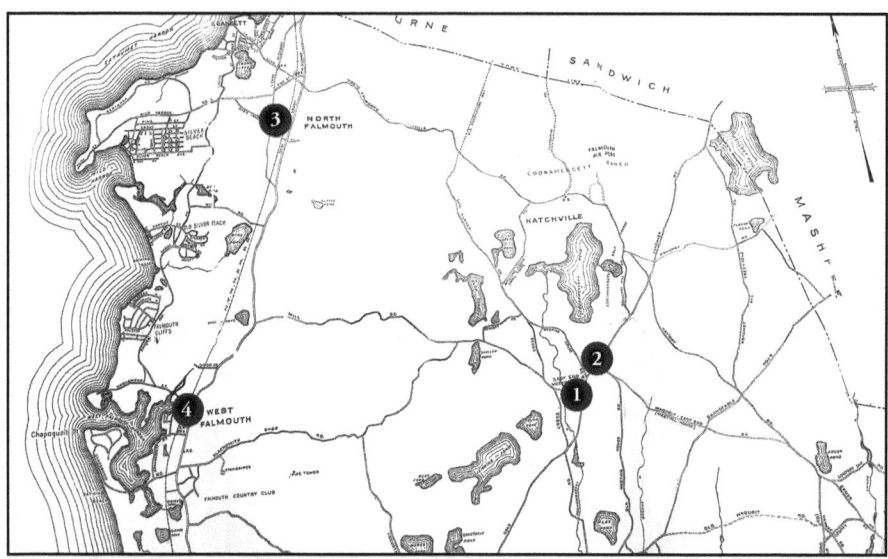

North Falmouth

Name of Bell	Location	Map Ref	Chapter Index	Foundry	Type	Dia in	Wgt lbs	Date
East End Meetinghouse	East End Meetinghouse	1	6,9	Hooper	church	38	983	1842
Falmouth Jewish Congregation	Falmouth Jewish Congregation	2	9	(Blake)	church	27	(400)	(1898)
North Falmouth Congregational	North Falmouth Congregational	3	6,8	Holbrook	church	(22)		1848
West Falmouth Methodist	West Falmouth Methodist	4	1,6,10	Blake/ Hooper	church	31	619	1871

74

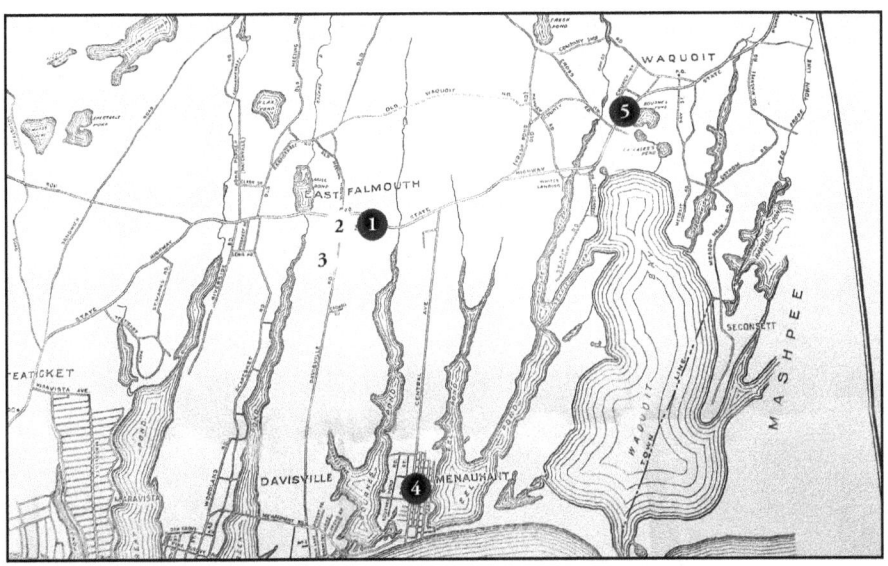

East Falmouth

Name of Bell	Location	Map Ref	Chapter Index	Foundry	Type	Dia in	Wgt lbs	Date
East Falmouth Fire - Hooper	East Falmouth Fire Station	1	7,10	Hooper	fire alarm	22.5	(250)	1855
East Falmouth Fire - truck	East Falmouth Fire Station	1	7,10	(unknown)	fire engine	9.5	(40)	(1915)
East Falmouth Methodist	(missing)	2	9,10	(unknown)	church			1898
East Falmouth School	(missing)	3	14	(unknown)	school	(18)		(1866)
Grace Memorial Chapel	Grace Memorial Chapel	4	2	(unknown)	church	(24)	(250)	(1931)
Waquoit Congregational	Waquoit Congregational	5	1,6	Hooper	church			1850

17

INSCRIPTIONS ON FALMOUTH BELLS

This chapter records the inscriptions found on the bells. The order of listing corresponds to the Maps and Facts chapter.

DOWNTOWN

FALMOUTH MARINE PARK

U.S.L.H.E.

FIRE DEPT 9/11

(none)

FIRE DEPT AMARAL

*Deputy Clifford Amaral,
gone but not forgotten*

FIRE DEPT ROBBINS

*Dedicated to Fire Chief Russell Robbins,
May 20, 1956 to May 16, 1986*

FIRE DEPT BRIGGS

*In memory of Reuben F Briggs
1976 – 1979*

First Congregational

The living to the church I call, and to the grave I summon all

Lawrence Academy

G. H. H. Mass 1835

North Falmouth School

(none)

St. Barnabas garden

Meneely Bell Company
Troy, N.Y. U.S.A.
Lawrence High School 1895

St. Barnabas tower

Blake Bell Co. Presented to
St. Barnabas. Falmouth.
By J. Arthur Beebe.
Boston Mass. 1891.

Union Chapel

Union Chapel Association,
Falmouth Heights,
Mass., 1906.
P.D. Cowan, president,
A.C.Munroe, Sec-Treas,
One Lord, One Faith, One Baptism

Woods Hole Methodist

Peoples M. E. Church
Pastor R. H. Dorr
July 1884.
Henry McShane & CO.
Baltimore Md 1884

Woods Hole

Bell tower, Mendel

I will teach you of life – and of life eternal
Gillett & Johnston
Croydon, England. 1929.

Bell tower, Pasteur

Pasteur
Thanks be to God
Gillett & Johnston,
Croydon, England. 1929.

Church of Messiah

Cast by Henry N Hooper Company
Boston 1854

Lightship

(missing)

RV Chain

USS Chain 1944

References

SPOHR GARDENS, BRONZE

Cast by William Blake and Co,
formerly H.N.Hooper & Co
Boston Mass 1882
Sinners! The sound of this bell calls you together
for the good and eternal happiness of your souls
and to praise and glorify Christ and only this
This bell is consecrated to truth
presented to the Baptist church in East Dedham Mass
by Jonathan Mann
Feb 20 1882

SPOHR GARDENS, STEEL

(none)

WOODS HOLE CONGREGATIONAL

McShane Bell Foundry
Baltimore MD, 1890
The Gift of Love H Davis to
The First Congregational Church of Woods Holl
As a Memorial of Her Husband Jabez Davis
of Woods Holl who died April 1st 1889

WOODS HOLE SCHOOL

(none)

NORTH FALMOUTH

EAST END MEETINGHOUSE

Cast by Henry N Hooper & Co
Boston 1842

FALMOUTH JEWISH CONGREGATION

(none)

NORTH FALMOUTH CONGREGATIONAL

Cast by G H Holbrook
Medway Mass 1848

WEST FALMOUTH METHODIST

Cast by William Blake & Co.
Formerly H. N. Hooper & Co.
Boston Mass. 1871

East Falmouth

East Falmouth Fire – Hooper

*Cast by Henry N Hooper Company
Boston 1855*

East Falmouth Fire – truck

(none)

East Falmouth Methodist

(missing)

East Falmouth School

(missing)

Grace Memorial Chapel

(none)

Waquoit Congregational

*Hooper & Company
Boston 1850*

Acknowledgments

I am happy to recognize some of the people and institutions that helped me prepare this book.

Bill Hough at the *Falmouth Enterprise* accepted my stories and gave me encouragement. When he retired, John Hough continued the support including access to their quirky but irreplaceable paper archives.

I made extensive use of Falmouth Public Library's Digital Collections that give online access to the *Enterprise* newspaper and the Town of Falmouth Annual reports. The postcard collection and School Yearbooks were also useful.

Carl Zimmerman, renowned bell expert, has been a mentor and a constant source of information and perspective. His website and reference information are justifiably recognized worldwide, and his editorial expertise was greatly appreciated.

Neil Goeppinger is an amazing and reliable source of a broad spectrum of bell information.

Closer to home Meg Costello at the Falmouth Historical Society has always been willing to locate items and open the archives to me.

Colleen Hurter at the Woods Hole Historical Museum helped me find many things at their lively small museum.

My son, Richard Peal, gave me the benefit of his experience in the publishing industry that was mostly new information to me.

I. Michael Grossman of EBookBakery Books very generously guided me through the process of preparing and editing a book. He has offered extensive advice and technical insights that made the book better at many levels.

Finally, many other friends and contacts in town who have listened to me and made helpful suggestions are much appreciated.

About the Author

Kenneth Peal was born and educated in Canada and emigrated with his young family to Falmouth in 1971 to take a job as an electrical engineer at the Woods Hole Oceanographic Institution. During many years at WHOI, his work changed from the early days of learning how to use room-sized computers at sea to designing and deploying underwater instruments that often have several computers inside a small pressure case. His travels to test and deploy these instruments took him on ships to most of the world's oceans and to the high arctic where he lived in ice camps for several weeks at a time.

Now retired, he volunteers around town and actively follows his interest in things historic and environmental. One of his hobbies is "fixing things that were never meant to be fixed" to fight against the throwaway society.

He lives with his wife, Michele, in a 160-year old house on Cape Cod which he happily opens to his children and grandchildren especially during the summer.

REFERENCES

General note on the references that follow:

The website www.towerbells.org is an unsurpassed resource for bell information of all kinds. It is the personal project of Carl Zimmerman, a widely recognized expert about the many worlds of bells.

Neil Goeppinger's book, *Large Bells of America, History of Church Bells, Fire Bells, School Bells, Dinner Bells, and Their Foundries*, Suncoast Digital Press Inc., Sarasota, Florida, 2016 fulfills the promise of its title. Additions and corrections to this book can be found at www.towerbells.org.

Wikipedia text is used under the Creative Commons Deed Creative Commons Attribution-ShareAlike License 3.0. Full terms of the license are at https://creativecommons.org/licenses/by-sa/3.0/.

Falmouth Annual Reports references were retrieved from the Olive Software archives which cover publications from 1896 to 1962.

Falmouth Enterprise references were retrieved from the Olive Software archives which cover publications from 1896 to 1962 or from Falmouth History Archives Online which covers publications from 1896 to 2017

The Olive Software project was made possible by a grant funded by the Community Preservation Committee under the Community Preservation Act in 2013.

Cape Cod Times references were retrieved from microfilm at the Falmouth Public Library.

CHAPTER 1 - FINDING BELLS IN FALMOUTH
(None)

CHAPTER 2 - UNION CHAPEL
1 – Candace Jenkins, "The Development of Falmouth as a Summer Resort 1850-1900", Woods Hole Historical Museum, *Spritsail*, volume 6, number 1, 1992, page 10
2 – "Falmouth Heights", *Falmouth Enterprise*, January 3, 1929, 2
3 – "Falmouth Locals", *Falmouth Enterprise*, July 17, 1897, 1
4 – "Falmouth Heights", *Falmouth Enterprise*, August 30, 1902, 8
5 – "Additional Falmouth Locals", *Falmouth Enterprise*, July 26, 1902, 4
6 – "Falmouth Heights", *Falmouth Enterprise*, August 6, 1904, 2
7 – "Falmouth Heights", *Falmouth Enterprise*, August 16, 1913, 3
8 – "Falmouth Heights", *Falmouth Enterprise*, July 1, 1905, 8
9 – "Falmouth Heights", *Falmouth Enterprise*, August 26, 1905, 5
10 – "Falmouth Heights", *Falmouth Enterprise*, July 7, 1906, 6
11 – "Falmouth Heights", *Falmouth Enterprise*, July 25, 1914, 6
12 – "Falmouth Heights", *Falmouth Enterprise*, July 18, 1925, 9
13 – "Falmouth Heights", *Falmouth Enterprise*, January 3, 1929, 2
14 – "Falmouth Heights", *Falmouth Enterprise*, January 24, 1929, 2
15 – "Commonwealth of Massachusetts", *Falmouth Enterprise*, January 31, 1929, 6

16 – "To Remove Chapel", *Falmouth Enterprise*, April 11, 1929, 8
17 – "Falmouth Heights", *Falmouth Enterprise*, August 29, 1929, 9

CHAPTER 3 - THE CHAMBER OF COMMERCE BELL
18 - National Register of Historic Places National, Archives Identifier 63794049, section 8 page 6
19 – "Academy Bell Added To Museum", *Falmouth Enterprise*, May 20, 1938, 3
20 - National Register of Historic Places National, Archives Identifier 63794049, section 8, page 6
21 - A National List of Holbrook Bells,
 https://www.chepachetbaptist.org/national-list-holbrook-bells.htm, retrieved April 2023
22 - Robert Elphick, *Falmouth Past and Present*, Kendall Printing Co., Falmouth, MA, 1958, page 42
23 – "Alumni Reception And Dance", *Falmouth Enterprise*, June 22, 1907, 8
24 – "The Sound Breezes Whisper", *Falmouth Enterprise*, November 16, 1918, 2
25 – Declaration of Restrictions recorded with the Barnstable County Registry of Deeds, "Book 30374, page 176, 27 Mar 2017", page 1, section 3, Covenant to Maintain
26 – Declaration of Restrictions recorded with the Barnstable County Registry of Deeds, "Book 30374, page 176, 27 Mar 2017", Exhibit B - Restriction Guidelines, page 21
27 – "Old Weathervane" (picture), *Falmouth Enterprise*, May 9, 1975, 7
28 – "Bells To Ring On The Fourth", *Falmouth Enterprise*, April 27, 1976, 7
29 - Robert Elphick, *Falmouth Past and Present*, Kendall Printing Co., Falmouth, MA, 1958, page 43
30 - National Register of Historic Places National, Archives Identifier 63794049. section 8 page 6

CHAPTER 4 - FOG
31 - Thomas Tag, "Fog Bells", U.S. Lighthouse Society Archive, https://uslhs.org/fog-bells, retrieved April 2023, used by permission
32 - History of WHOI Ships, Chain, 1958-1979, https://www.whoi.edu/multimedia/v-history-of-whoi-ships/, retrieved April 2023, used by permission
33 - The WHOI archives (https://www.dla.whoi.edu/) contain many "linear feet" of boxes containing "cruise summaries, crew lists, correspondence, and other files" relating to Chain 99. To my knowledge there is no single, definitive publication of this ground breaking cruise.
34 - USS Chain (ARS-20), https://en.wikipedia.org/wiki/USS_Chain_(ARS-20), retrieved April 2023
35 - Wayne Wheeler, "History of the Administration of the Lighthouses in America", U.S. Lighthouse Society Archive, https://uslhs.org/history-administration-lighthouses-america, retrieved April 2023, used by permission
36 - Nobska Point (Massachusetts), Historical Light List Audible Fog Signals, U.S. Lighthouse Society Archive, https://uslhs.org/light_lists/lighthouse_list.php?id=1039, retrieved April 2023, used by permission
37 - Hudson Mohawk Industrial Gateway, Troy, NY, Spreadsheet of Entries in Troy Meneely Ledger Book, line 3096, from https://hudsonmohawkgateway.org/s/meneely_ledger.xls, retrieved April 2023, used by permission
38 - Boston Lightship LV54 WAL 502, http://www.uscglightshipsailors.org/boston_lightship_lv54_wal_502.htm, retrieved April 2023, used by permission

CHAPTER 5 - SPOHR
39 - https://spohrgardens.org/
40 - Personal communication 11 Apr 2023, with Beth Heinrich, Office Manager at Fellowship Bible Church, the successor to the Dedham Baptist Church
41 – "DEDHAM 1882 Church Bell.docx" retrieved from https://spohrgardens.org/ February 2021
42 – Cincinnati Bell Foundry Company's 1904 catalog, page 19
From the Collection of Cincinnati & Hamilton County Public Library, used by permission

CHAPTER 6 - CONGREGATIONAL BELLS
43 - Congregationalism in the United States, Disestablishment, https://en.wikipedia.org/wiki/Congregationalism_in_the_United_States#Disestablishment, retrieved April 2023
44 – Conversation with Jonathan Drury, 29th pastor of First Congregational Church of Falmouth, 9 May 2017

45 – First Congregational Church of Falmouth, Our History, https://firstcongregationalfalmouth.org/about-us, retrieved April 2023
46 – Lennie Conley, *A Brief Guide to the History of Falmouth, Cape Cod* United Church Apartments, undated, held in Falmouth Public Library reference section
47 – "Falmouth Historical Society", *Falmouth Enterprise*, October 13, 1900, 8
48 - Simeon L. Deyo, ed, *History of Barnstable County, Massachusetts, 1620 – 1890*, New York: H. W. Blake and Co., 1890, page 647
49 – https://www.falmouthjewish.org/about/, retrieved Apr 2023
50 - Simeon L. Deyo, ed, *History of Barnstable County, Massachusetts, 1620 – 1890*, New York: H. W. Blake and Co., 1890, page 649
51 – Waquoit Congregational Church, Our Story, https://waquoitchurch.org/wordpress/?page_id=130, retrieved Apr 2023
52 – CP Fund, Falmouth, "complete project list", https://www.cpfundfalmouth.org/historic-preservation-projects, Article A9, Apr 2009, retrieved Apr 2023

CHAPTER 7 - WALKING TOUR OF WOODS HOLE
53 - Simeon L. Deyo, ed, *History of Barnstable County, Massachusetts, 1620 – 1890*, New York: H. W. Blake and Co., 1890, page 650
54 – "Woods Hole Historical Collection Register, Woods Hole Congregational Church" from Woods Hole Historical Museum, Woods Hole, MA
55 – "ABC Hears Three Falmouth Liquor License Appeals", *Falmouth Enterprise*, April 30, 1948, 1
56 – "Moving Of Woods Hole Church Is Discussed", *Falmouth Enterprise*, February 25, 1949, 1
57 – Chestnut blight, https://en.wikipedia.org/w/index.php?title=Chestnut_blight&oldid=1144491761, retrieved Apr 2023
58 – "Summer School Of Science Bell Has Beckoned Since 1914", *Falmouth Enterprise*, August 30, 1991, 13
59 – "Engineer's Home-Made Mechanism Rings Bells In Woods Hole Tower", *Falmouth Enterprise*, July 24, 1953, 6a
60 – Jane A. McLaughlin, "The Angelus Bell Tower and Mary Garden in Woods Hole", Woods Hole Historical Museum, *Spritsail* volume 6, number 2, 1992, page 18, note 36
61 – "Enthusiastic Crew Cares For The Mary Garden", *Falmouth Enterprise*, January 1, 2021, 1-2
62 – "Woods Hole Historical Collection Register, Woods Hole Congregational Church" from Woods Hole Historical Museum, Woods Hole, MA

CHAPTER 8 - NORTH FALMOUTH
63 – https://nfcc.wildapricot.org/history, retrieved April 2023
64 – "Reflections on fourteen decades", in the North Falmouth Congregational Church records, 17.11.1 N81.5 NORFCC. Courtesy of the Congregational Library & Archives, Boston, MA
65 - Marion Rawson Vuilleumier, *Churches on Cape Cod*, Sullwood Publishing, Taunton, MA, 1974 (out of print)
66 - Simeon L. Deyo, ed, *History of Barnstable County, Massachusetts, 1620 – 1890*, New York: H. W. Blake and Co., 1890, page 294
67 - R. A. Lovell, *Sandwich, A Cape Cod Town*, Town of Sandwich Massachusetts Archives and Historical Center, 1984, page 292
68 – Unitarian Universalism, https://en.wikipedia.org/wiki/Unitarian_Universalism, retrieved April 2023
69 - R. A. Lovell, *Sandwich, A Cape Cod Town*, Town of Sandwich Massachusetts Archives and Historical Center, 1984, page 272
70 - R. A. Lovell, *Sandwich, A Cape Cod Town*, Town of Sandwich Massachusetts Archives and Historical Center, 1984, page 290
71 – A National List of Holbrook Bells, https://www.chepachetbaptist.org/national-list-holbrook-bells.htm, retrieved April 2023
72 – Personal communication, May 2023 from Dave Hewey, architect of the restoration
73 - D. Hamilton Hurd, *History of Hillsborough County, New Hampshire*, Philadelphia: J. W. Lewis & Co, 1885, page 334

134 – Stickney Bell Research Collection, Paul Revere Memorial Association, Boston, MA
135 – Stickney Bell Research Collection, Paul Revere Memorial Association, Boston, MA
136 – Minutes of the Falmouth Historical Society Annual Meeting, September 5, 1900
137 – "An Old Relic", *Falmouth Enterprise*, February 28, 1914, 5
138 – Groveland Historical Society, Paul Revere Bell, https://grovelandhistoricalsociety.org/history/historical-sites/paul-revere-bell/, retrieved April 2023

CHAPTER 14 - EAST FALMOUTH SCHOOL
139 – "School Bell Is Dedicated Memorial To Rita Carey", *Falmouth Enterprise*, November 17, 1967, 3
140 – Massachusetts Historical Commission, MGL chapter 40, section 8D, Form B, East Falmouth School, 470 East Falmouth Highway
141 – "New School Building", *Falmouth Annual Reports*, January 1, 1922, 5-7
142 – Barnstable County Registry of Deeds, 405-94, 12-12-1923
143 – "The Case For A New School", *Falmouth Enterprise*, November 9, 1956, 20
144 – "Gathering Honors Howard Barrows; Playground Will Be Named For Him", *Falmouth Enterprise*, June 11, 1965, 1
145 – Massachusetts Historical Commission, MGL chapter 40, section 8D, Form B, Davisville School, 406 Davisville Road
146 – "Davisville", *Falmouth Annual Reports*, December 31, 1884, 16
147 - Mary Lou Smith, ed, *The Book of Falmouth, A Tricentennial Celebration: 1686-1986*, The Falmouth Historical Commission, 1986, page 164,165
148 – Barnstable County Registry of Deeds, 449-184, 08-25-1927
149 – "Falmouth Sees New School As Chairman Pattee Gets Huge Key", *Falmouth Enterprise*, October 6, 1932, 1

INDEX

Symbols

9/11 46, 72, 77

A

Allenby, R. Gilbert 47
Amaral, Clifford 46, 77
American Bell Association 69
American Unitarian Association 36

B

Baker Monument Company 50
Barrows, Howard 61
Bates, Katharine Lee 12, 51
Beebe, E. Pierson 48
Blake Bell Co. 40, 78
Blymyer Manufacturing Company 20
Briggs, Grafton 4
Briggs, Reuben F 46, 77
Brown, Henry 43, 50
Brown, Lynne 59, 62
Bumpus, Catherine 17, 32, 33, 44
Butler, Martha 57

C

Cardoza, Jim 41
Chase, Tom 33, 47
CETA 13
Chain 15, 16, 17, 87
Chain, RV 15, 16, 73, 79
Chain, USS 16, 79, 87
Chepachet Baptist Church 37
Children's School of Science 32, 62
Church of the Messiah 29, 73
CIN BELL CO 20
clapper 3, 4, 13, 19, 43, 44, 66, 67
Clarkin, Charlie 44, 45
Cockerham, Walter 47
Cocks, Harry 47
C S Bell 69

D

Dorr, Pastor R. H. 1, 79
Drury, Reverend Jonathan 24, 36, 55, 87

E

East End Meeting House 25, 42
East Parish Meeting House 37
Endicott, Greg 13

F

Falmouth Enterprise vi, 8, 13, 33, 40, 43, 48, 52, 57, 59, 83, 86, 87, 88, 89, 90, 91, 93
Falmouth Heights Land and Wharf Company 7
Falmouth Historical Society vii, 13, 49, 52, 55, 57, 62, 71, 83, 90
Falmouth's Community Preservation Fund 26
Fellowship Bible Church 20
First Catholic Church Patchogue 20
First Congregational Church 1, 23, 24, 25, 28, 31, 36, 55, 80, 87

G

Gifford, James 44, 89
Gillett and Johnston 32, 69
Grace Memorial Chapel 7, 75, 82
Green, A. R. 41
Greenfield's Union Congregational Church 38
Groveland Congregational Church 58

H

Hamilton Tree Co. 5, 28
Hannaford, C. S. 10
Harris, Mabel S. 10
Henry McShane & Co 2
Henry N Hooper & company 25
Hilton, Sumner 44, 89
H. N. Hooper & Co 20, 81
Hobart, Aaron 68
Holbrook, George H. 12, 51
Hurter, Colleen, 45, 83

J

John Wesley Church 1, 4, 31, 41, 72, 89

K

King's Chapel 56

L

Lawrence, H. V. 41
Lawrence Academy iv, 11, 12, 51, 57, 72, 78
Leipzig 4
Liberty Bell 4, 69
Liberty Hall 44

M

MacKilligan, Joseph 49
Menauhant Chapel 7
Meneely Bell Company 9, 51, 78
Methodist Society Burying Ground 41
Mills, Greg 55
Mullen-Hall 53, 54

N

New Bedford Standard Times 41
New England Fire and History Museum 46
Nichols, Arthur H 56
North Falmouth Church 36, 37, 38
North Falmouth School 62, 72, 78

P

Paul Revere bell 1, 23, 24, 25, 43, 55, 58, 90
Paul Revere Day 55
Peal, Ken 85

R

Redfield, Dr A. C. 31
Rose, John 43, 44

S

Slater, Bob 26
Second Congregational Church 25
Seth Thomas clock 24, 55, 58
Smith, Cynthia 41, 42
Smythe, Rev Henry Herbert 49
Spohr Gardens iv, 1, 19, 20, 21, 73, 80

Spritsail 43, 44, 45, 49, 86, 88, 89, 90, 93
St. Barnabas Episcopal iv, 1, 47
Stickney, Edward 56, 57, 69
Stickney, Evelyn 56, 69, 90
St Thomas Chapel 7

T

toller 66

U

Union Chapel iv, 7, 8, 9, 72, 78
Union Chapel Association 9, 78
Unitarian Universalist Association 36
USLHE 17, 18, 72

V

Verdin Company of Cincinnati 33
Vose, John 30

W

Waquoit Congregational 1, 26, 27, 75, 82, 88
Waquoit Congregational Church 26, 27, 88
West Falmouth Methodist 1, 25, 44, 74, 81
Westminster chimes 66
Wheeler & Co. 18
White, Olivia 55
WHOI 1, 3, 15, 16, 17, 31, 73, 85, 87, 93
Woods Hole black 29
Woods Hole Congregational 30, 73, 80, 88
Woods Hole Historical Museum vii, 29, 30, 31, 44, 83, 86, 88, 89, 90, 93
Woods Hole Methodist Church 2, 3, 31

Y

Yankee Steeplejack Co 26

Z

Zimmerman, Carl 42, 57, 83, 86, 89

www.ingramcontent.com/pod-product-compliance
Lightning Source LLC
Chambersburg PA
CBHW072202100426
42738CB00011BA/2505